Educational sciences

The theory of curriculum content in the USSR

V.V. Kraevskij
I.Y. Lerner

Prepared for the
International Bureau
of Education

8482

In the series 'Educational sciences':

Landsheere, G. De. *Empirical research in education.* 1982. 113 p.

Zverev, I.D. *Teaching methods in the Soviet school.* 1983. 116 p.

Kraevskij, V.V.; Lerner, I.Y. *The theory of curriculum content in the USSR.* 1984.

Published by the United Nations
Educational, Scientific and Cultural Organization,
7, place de Fontenoy, 75700 Paris, France.

ISBN: 92-3-102128-1

Printed in Switzerland by Atar S.A., Geneva.

Preface

This book is the third monograph in the series on educational sciences. Its subject is of theoretical and practical interest since the problem of curriculum content at various levels and in different types of education remains a contemporary educational issue in the context of the rapid evolution of societies and the advancement of science and technology. The school and the teachers have too often been blamed for providing education that is irrelevant to the needs of children and to the aspirations of society, as well as for the lack of interest in studies on the part of the children — and for the poor results of teaching and learning in general. The authors of this book attempt to show that one of the reasons for this shortcoming is the absence of a scientific foundation for constructing curriculum content which, in the past, has often been developed in a piecemeal way and based on the subjective opinions of curriculum designers.

For a number of years the research institutes of the Academy of Pedagogical Sciences of the USSR, in collaboration with school-teachers, have been working towards the establishment of a theory of curriculum content. V.V. Kraevskij, a corresponding member of the Academy of Pedagogical Sciences of the USSR, and I.Y. Lerner, doctor of educational sciences, who both work at the Research Institute of General Pedagogics in Moscow, have made a substantial contribution to the development of this theory. Their book is a first-hand account of the results achieved and the problems encountered. Several of their previous publications were in fact guidelines for those dealing with the construction of curriculum content or manuals for teachers on the practical application of the theory. It is hoped that this book, although its theme is a theory, will be of interest to a much broader readership than specialists in educational research. All those who deal in one way or another with curriculum development will find the following analysis useful.

We wish to express our cordial thanks to both authors for their invaluable and efficient contribution to the International Bureau of Education's series on the educational sciences. However, we would point out that the ideas and opinions expressed in this book are those of the authors and do not necessarily represent the views of Unesco, while the designations employed and the presentation of the material throughout the publication do not imply the expression of any opinion whatsoever on the part of Unesco concerning the legal status of any country, territory, city or area or of its authorities, or concerning the delimitations of its frontiers or boundaries.

Contents

Introduction

Among the numerous problems confronting the modern school, some are recurrent ones depending for solution on the adoption of decisions of principle concerning virtually every aspect of the development of the public education system. Such problems concern increasing the effectiveness of teaching in general and the performance of pupils in particular, as well as the methods, techniques and organization of instruction. At the same time, it is fair to distinguish between practical difficulties and such theoretical problems as are likely to contribute to their solution. The theoretical problems are above all associated with the compilation of the content of secondary education and with the means of expressing this content in materials used by teachers and pupils in their daily work — curricula, textbooks and teaching manuals.

In many countries educationists have been focusing their attention upon the development of a theory of curriculum construction. Its purpose is not merely to elucidate curriculum content but also the teaching process and, of course, the goals to be attained, which during compulsory education must be obligatory.

Even in countries with a decentralized system of education, considerable importance is attached to the definition of core curricula, i.e. that minimum of knowledge which is expected of all pupils.

It is the mass, compulsory nature of modern secondary school education that makes the availability of an adequate theory underlying the construction of curriculum content a matter of first priority. However, such a theory cannot be limited to setting goals for general education. These goals have to be adapted to the educational situation prevailing in actual classroom conditions. And to make this possible one should examine the potential of actual schools, teachers and pupils. One should also inquire into those laws, principles and methods which govern the educational process, i.e. to the total of components that influence teaching.

Whenever the goals of education are restated on a new theoretical basis, special attention should be given to the prevailing situation in the context of instruction, i.e. to educational reality. More often than not, that reality itself has been subject to piecemeal changes. Sooner or later a gap arises between the goals and results of educational activity. This gap — common to all education systems — results in school-leavers failing to meet the expected academic standards. There is a tendency to blame this ostensible failure both on the educationist and the teacher, the former for impractical theories and the latter for being negligent in his duty to inculcate knowledge and standards of behaviour. Such disparity between theory and practice, however, should only serve to motivate the educationist to try still harder in his search for proposals that would amend the situation.

At such times the educationist's ability to forestall events is put to the test. It is incumbent upon a theorist to learn to predict, after a bare minimum of experience, how the projected educational theory will measure up with new conditions, how it will adapt to them, thus partly filling the gap between goals set and results achieved.

Whatever the guidelines and the scholastic realities of compulsory secondary education may be in each particular case, effective results in any education system are attainable only if the content of education in curricular and textbook form, from its very inception, has taken proper account not merely of the goals of education, but also of the possibilities of their implementation.

Now our discourse has reached a point when it is absolutely essential to provide ourselves with a *modus operandi*. Indeed, *how* does one take proper account of educational goals? How are these goals co-ordinated with particular school subjects? How should one distribute them properly over the curriculum and syllabuses? How does one take proper account of teaching conditions? How should the content of study material be contrived so that it is neither too easy nor too difficult for the pupil to acquire? What are the criteria to follow?

Providing adequate answers to these questions is likely to benefit all educators, and above all, the compilers of textbooks and study materials. The answers should be fairly comprehensive and properly evaluated. One should beware of short-cuts or easy answers. A useful theory must be based on sound premises. It would be unrealistic to expect a panacea. The answers may even appear paradoxical, but a scientific truth simply cannot be self-evident; its real value is in fostering new ideas. If such a theory were available, it would be quite realistic to expect that one would be able to forecast with reasonable certainty how a given lesson in a given subject will be imparted to and acquired by the pupils. Even though an educational theory cannot pretend to ward off all the errors resulting from the inadequate planning of teaching, one could expect a theory to help the teacher avoid major blunders.

In the period of transition to universal compulsory education — at first in the junior secondary (seven-year) school and then in the complete, secondary (formerly ten-year now eleven-year) school — Soviet teachers and educationists gained much experience in solving some very challenging problems. They have been faced with a further set of complicated practical and theoretical problems as a result of the most recent reform of secondary education. The book we are introducing to the reader purports to analyse solutions to these problems in retrospect, as far as they are of consequence to the development of content for general secondary education and as far as they contribute to a scientific substantiation of that content. Considerable space is devoted to the general principles now being developed by the Research Institute of General Pedagogics of the USSR Academy of Pedagogical Sciences.

The developers are primarily concerned with three groups of problems.

The first group comprises *problems of methodology*. So far, a new approach to the development of a theory for the content of general education has been identified and implemented. It forms part of a broader educational theory based on the principles of general philosophy and on the data collected in an effort to devise a methodology for such a theory. First and foremost, a theory for the content of general secondary education should result from the definition of that content both from the stance of the educational sciences and that of general social goals and requirements. Curriculum content is examined in terms of the educational sciences with due regard to the usual forms it takes in educational situations.

A theory of curriculum content is being developed with due regard to its dissemination in the schools. Such attention to practical application in no way contradicts the general trend for a more profound theoretical approach. Neither is this utilitarian approach to be equated with an unsophisticated substitution of practice for theory. No matter how abstract a theory may be, it cannot but reflect some aspects of its practical application. Whatever the degree of abstraction of an educational theory, provided it is truly educational, it must of necessity retain the major characteristics of *educational reality*, i.e. a situation which takes the form of educational activity. Whatever is part of educational activity is also part of educational reality. Thus, a flower as such is not part of educational reality, yet, it can be made part of it by including information on the plant in an appropriate textbook and hence in the process of education.

The content of education, if the above approach is consistently followed, should conform as far as possible to the process by which it is implemented, i.e. the day-to-day classroom environment in which teachers teach and pupils learn.

The second group includes *fundamental problems concerning a theory of curriculum content*. These are problems associated with determining the composition of this content, i.e. its elements. The elemental composition of curriculum content in the particular case of the socialist school is determined by the goal of the comprehensive development of the personality, which means the acquirement of certain intellectual, moral, political, vocational, aesthetic and physical qualities. The content of general secondary education cannot be reduced to an inventory of scientific facts, skills and habits to be acquired in the matrix of a particular branch of knowledge or subject. Of necessity it includes the basic elements of social experience, the acquisition of which are essential for every member of society.

Other problems associated with a theory concern the structure of curriculum content, its sources, as well as the composition, construction and classification of school subjects.

The third group includes problems associated with the *development of definite norms and recommendations upon which to base curriculum content*. The above norms may cover a wide range of notions differing in the degree of application: from the general principles which underlie the development of curriculum content to the particular demands placed upon curriculum and textbook development. This group of problems is likewise of significance, since being a theory of activity, an educational theory must by definition have its own specifics and consequently cannot be constructed merely on the grounds of a scientific theory which may exclude practical activity from its composition. In this respect, we agree[1] with those authors, such as Hirst, who maintain that 'value assessments that are significant in deciding to do A rather than B must be made from within [the theory] and are not simply derivable from value assessments taken from without'[2].

In this book, interest is limited to a few basic theoretical problems of curriculum content and possible approaches to their solution.

The introduction, Chapter I and Section 1 of Chapter III were written by V.V. Kraevskij; Chapter II and Sections 2 to 4 of Chapter III were written mainly by I.Ya. Lerner but with some additional material by V.V. Kraevskij.

REFERENCES

1.   Kraevskij, V.V *Problemy naučnogo obosnovanija obučenija (metodologičeskij analiz).* Moskva, 'Pedagogika', 1977. 264 p.

2.   Hirst, P.H. The nature and scope of educational theory. *In*: Langford, G.; O'Connor, J.D., eds. *New essays in the philosophy of education.* Boston, Mass., Routledge & Kegan Paul, 1973, p. 71.

CHAPTER I
The content of general secondary education: theory and problems

1. CONTENT OF EDUCATION AS AN EDUCATIONAL PROBLEM

Even today, Lenin's principles of public education in general and communist education in particular remain fundamental in determining the goals and content of Soviet general education: educational content in line with the new goals of education, contributing to the solution of important social issues whether political, economic or cultural; a redefinition of the foundations of general education; and the provision of a new theory for the content of formal education.

An important contribution to the theory of general education from the very beginning was the principle of one school for all, which provided for a system under which every school boy and girl could enter higher education. The very idea of the so-called terminal education existing in many other countries has always been foreign to the Soviet education system.

With the gradual development of society, the role of general education has become more important. This is especially true of a new socialist society. Indeed, it is in the process of education, the process of imparting the content of general education, that young people acquire the foundations of science, culture and art, the principles of a scientific worldview, socially acceptable morals and behaviour, and basic manual skills and habits. It is through this process that the pupil learns to think for himself and acquires a creative approach to the work he is doing.

In socialist society, both comprehensive and polytechnical branches of study serve to inculcate in the learner the awareness of being in charge of his own life, a personality in his own right and, at the same time, to qualify him for a particular job, be it manual or intellectual. This role of education in the development of society and in the creation of a new man is precisely in the spirit of Lenin's view of the content of general education.

Lenin's concept of general education has materialized today in the public education system of the USSR to include an extensive network of pre-school institutions, secondary general education schools, vocational training and secondary specialized educational establishments, colleges and universities, not forgetting facilities catering for out-of-school activities. This system, the advantages of which have by now become known throughout the world, guarantees the learner an excellent standard of education. The content of education in the USSR is constantly aligned with current social, technological and scientific developments.

Irrespective of the type of school, educational content is prescribed by a uniform curriculum which is based on the principles of Soviet formal education. With the objective of comprehensive personality development, the curriculum stands guard over the structural unity and continuity of educational content. Accordingly, each pupil is expected to acquire a specified minimum of knowledge, irrespective of the type of secondary school he attends or his aptitude. Upon finishing the eight-year school, the pupil is free to continue education either in comprehensive school or any other type of secondary establishment. The school curriculum in the USSR is based on the principle of the interdependence of comprehensive and polytechnical learning and vocational guidance. Considerable time is set aside for manual and physical training, as well as aptitude testing to enable the pupil to choose the subject which suits him or her best.

Whatever its type, the school in the USSR offers a wide range of humanities and natural science subjects. Since its inception, more classroom time has been allotted for the humanities than the natural sciences. Included under the humanities are languages, literature, history, social science, geography, study of the constitution, elements of state and law, drawing and music; while mathematics, physics, chemistry, biology, astronomy, technical drawing and natural history comprise the natural sciences. Of course, the Soviet school also offers manual training and physical education[1].

The education system and its content keep pace with the country's progress. Major contributions to educational science and practice from the past were the establishment of a link between formal education, daily life and productive work, the adoption of the principle of all-round development of the personality and a more precise definition of how school subjects should reflect the content of the corresponding sciences.

In conformity with the curricula of the early 1920s, from his first day at school the pupil was imparted with the idea that work is the chief purpose in life, an idea to be developed in subsequent years of study. The contemplative and passive view of nature was rejected in favour of the idea of harnessing the forces of nature in the interests of the working population. In short, the keynote of these curricula was a nature/work/society formula. The curricula sought to give the younger generation an overview of the world at large and to inculcate an attitude of social participation.

In the 1930s, with the growing demand for trained specialists, new school curricula and syllabuses were compiled as a contribution to improving the standards of general education. The time had come to put into practice the universal goals of school education in day-to-day teaching. Makarenko, the eminent educationist, wrote on this subject: 'The results of our work will be no better than the qualities of the human beings we are now moulding with a professional hand'[2].

In developing techniques for basic policies, some educationists came to the conclusion that educational goals could be best formulated as an inventory of problems for secondary school pupils to learn and solve in the course of their studies. The process of defining educational goals was conceived as a step-by-step procedure comprising identification, introduction according to an agreed pattern, and application in different circumstances (presenting an element of creativity). All these attempts to define goals essentially involved the setting of problems and the indication of possible approaches to their solution without, however, any consistent educational theory emerging.

From the early 1930s to the mid 1950s, the main thrust of Soviet formal education was upon the preparation of pupils for college and university with a view to accelerating progress in industry and to cater for the corresponding increase in demand for engineers and technicians. Yet, since the mid 1950s, it had become clear that this approach was no longer valid for determining the goals of the secondary school. The late 1950s were characterized by efforts to optimize the content of formal education. Among the vast variety of problems tackled at that time by theorists and innovators were: how economic, scientific, technological and cultural progress should be reflected in the content of education; how to deal with the new demands placed upon the socialization and education of the younger generation by that progress; the behavioural characteristics of pupils at different stages of education, etc. Apart from work on problems of general education at that period, profound studies were undertaken on such fundamental socio-educational problems as comprehensive personality development. Philosophers, economists and educationists were actively involved in these projects.

The period 1958-60 saw a further revision of educational content, involving changes in curricula and syllabuses, the introduction of in-service training and the transfer of the teaching of all the natural and exact sciences onto a polytechnical basis.

Yet, this partial updating of school curricula did not provide an adequate solution; what school-teachers and theorists had to do was to ensure that the content of formal education kept pace with technical, scientific and cultural progress, while at the same time achieving the successful transition to universal secondary learning. In 1964, the USSR Academy of Sciences and the RSFSR Academy of Pedagogical Sciences appointed a joint commission to determine the content of secondary school education.

Seated on the commission were distinguished scholars, educationists, methodologists, psychologists and prominent teachers. The commission carried out a sweeping curriculum/syllabus revision with regard to all school subjects.

Educational content was considerably enriched to reflect with greater fidelity scientific, technological and cultural progress. A much closer connection was established between the sciences as they are taught in school and the latest achievements in mathematics, physics, chemistry and biology, as well as in science and technology in general; greater emphasis was placed in the new curriculum upon orienting the pupils towards participation in socio-economic activities and, at the same time, on aesthetic and cultural personality development with a view to making work and life in Soviet society more inspiring and rewarding.

In recent years, educationists in the USSR have been concentrating on the development of methods of providing polytechnical education at a level which would satisfy the present and future requirements of the socio-political and economic progress of Soviet society.

It is incumbent upon polytechnical education, within the context of education in general, to introduce pupils to the scientific background of modern production processes, to teach them such general work skills as are readily applicable in new situations and to develop their initiative in solving technological, organizational and economic problems arising in actual productive work. Thus, polytechnical education is meant to contribute appreciably to the all-round and harmonious development of the pupils and to help resolve such socially vital problems as overcoming the substantial differences between manual and intellectual work, as well as the question of how to turn work into a source of enjoyment instead of drudgery.

Numerous studies have been made by Soviet educationists to identify a scientific foundation for the content of polytechnical education. For instance, one of these studies covered the work performed by craftsmen engaged in the most common trades in order to provide a basis for the skills to be acquired by the polytechnically educated person; this now serves as a guide for polytechnical education in secondary general education school. There are five principles to follow in updating production: mechanization; electrification; automation; organization; and efficiency. Besides the imparting of essential skills and abilities, polytechnical courses in school must reflect these five principles. Polytechnical education involves not only imparting to the pupils the fundamentals of science, but also providing them with in-service training and encouraging their active participation in socially useful work.

By learning the fundamentals of the natural sciences, the pupils become familiar with the laws of nature and the ways of applying them in production. The same is applicable to the social laws and principles which the pupils learn in the course of social sciences (history, social science proper and economic geography).

In their basic scientific course, the pupils learn to measure, calculate and draw, thus acquiring skills likely to be useful to them in actual work situations. They also learn to cope with the tasks and problems of applying scientific laws to production.

However, the content of polytechnical education does not end there. There are technological laws and basic rules of organization and economics of the work process that cannot be adequately taught in the elements-of-science course without violating the sequence of the learning process. Teaching these matters should rather be included in the theoretical portion of manual training.

On-the-job training involves the pupils directly in real situations which give them a foretaste of the working world. By actually participating in the solution of these problems and, as far as possible, in raising working efficiency and promoting socialist attitudes on the factory floor, the pupils learn to work as a team and adopt a creative approach to whatever they are assigned to do.

To improve the content of general education, we should first identify the main concepts and only then impart the whole body of material.

In the newly introduced mathematics syllabuses, closer connection was established between arithmetic and algebra, while the teaching of mathematics was made more functional.

The instruction of physics was more solidly based on molecular-atomic, molecular-kinetic and electron theories, the wave and quantum explanation of light, the theory of relativity and the modern understanding of atomic structure.

In the school course of chemistry, the periodic law is now taught in more junior forms, while the problems of chemical bonding and the dependence of properties on the structure of substances are treated in greater depth, the syllabus prescribing the basic characteristics of chemical processes (rate of reactions, shift in chemical balance) as well as a more profound presentation of protein properties and structure, the chemistry of nucleic acids and their role in the organism.

In botany and zoology more stress was laid upon the theory of evolution, ecology, histology, physiology, while in the syllabus of human anatomy and general biology more attention is given to the cell theory and genetics.

In the syllabuses of history and social science the special emphasis was on actual change in socio-economic structures and the role of people as a motive force in history.

The syllabus for literature is now focused upon the study of outstanding literary works, with more regard to the learner's age.

The purpose of optional courses provided in schools was to better reflect technical, scientific and cultural progress by offering to particularly enthusiastic pupils the possibility of an in-depth study of the subjects for which they showed a special preference.

The introduction of these curricula and syllabuses, as recommended by the commission, made a considerable contribution to the theoretical side of formal education.

However, the revised curricula were not altogether faultless. As a result of inadequate evaluation, some syllabuses and textbooks were overburdened with non-essentials.

The construction of an adequate educational content is no easy matter since it involves the preliminary solution of a number of strictly educational problems. Even the brief survey presented above shows that the theoretical problems associated with content construction are not new to Soviet educational science. In developing syllabuses and curricula, and the textbooks which are to reflect them, the educationists have had to tackle problems that can be solved only through an in-depth study and after the collection of sufficient data to enable a clear understanding of the issues involved. The concepts already arrived at are tested both on a large scale in schools and on a more restricted scale in specially designed experiments. Some of these concepts, upon further improvement and evaluation, have contributed to the development of a general theory of educational content; others have had to be discarded as erroneous. However, even the negative results have proved useful to researchers who are now able, by analysing their own failures, to have a clear understanding of the very process of definition, thus casting a more critical look on their own methodology for the selection and systematization of instructional material. As a result, curriculum planners have acquired new skills and more reliable reasoning for the solution of even more challenging problems.

Information on the methods of tackling problems of educational content in the USSR was conveyed to a meeting of Unesco experts in Moscow in 1967. These recommendations prescribed, *inter alia*, the method of selecting knowledge from the corresponding sciences to be included into the syllabuses for particular school subjects. The criteria for this process were: (a) the proven value of the material to be selected; (b) its social value; (c) its value in moulding a communist outlook; (d) the ease with which pupils can acquire it.

Upon analysing a particular subject with a view to selecting knowledge for inclusion in the syllabus, one may imagine it as a 'pyramid of concepts' with fundamental concepts at the summit, facts and phenomena at the foot; the higher the level the more abstract are the concepts.

This mental picture is useful in determining the proper place for each law, concept and fact in the matrix of a particular science and hence in selecting for the corresponding school subject primarily that material which elucidates the fundamental concepts.

To determine the degree to which the teaching of a particular school subject contributes to the attainment of the universal goals of socialization, instruction and harmonious development, the researchers have first to determine what society is actually expecting from the point of view of development of the personality. By analysing the prospects for social development, researchers have been able to forecast the pattern of activities and relationships — whether material, intellectual or social — which the prospective school graduates should possess on graduation. The researchers seek to identify those typical problems of knowledge and skills which the pupils are likely to face on finishing school, and those faculties and abilities which they will have to draw on in solving these problems. Educationists, together with psychologists, seek to understand the mechanisms of the development of abilities, judged by the acquisition of curriculum content, and the mechanisms of activity judged by knowledge acquisition and skill development. The system thus identified is then evaluated experimentally.

The development of the theoretical foundations of curriculum content goes hand-in-hand with efforts to improve it. Recently, important corrections have been made to existing curricula, as well as to some of the textbooks.

Babanskij has proposed an original criterion for selecting curriculum content from the corresponding science, which may be summarized as follows: 'It should be complex enough to meet modern scientific standards and simple enough to be understandable to the pupil, unified, acceptable in scientific terms, scientifically and socially useful, universally applicable and informative.'[3]

Today, there is a growing awareness among Soviet educationists of the need to construct curriculum content at a qualitatively higher level, taking advantage of the rich experience they have by now acquired. This is especially important now when the Soviet school is being reformed and new requirements are put forward to raise the quality of education imparted to the younger generation. The highest values of socialist society are placed on rapid and harmonious development of economics and culture in general and each individual's personality in particular. Apart from the in-depth study of particular problems that have been conducted by Soviet educationists, there arises a need for an integrated theory of educational content which would permit an overview of the situation. In a report to a plenary session of the USSR Academy of Pedagogical Sciences (1975) on the Soviet school's adoption of new educational content, Zverev, having noted good progress, pointed out that the largely inductive approach was still hampering the development of an integrated system of educational concepts to cover all aspects of the problem and he also added that the current level of educational theory was not satisfactory, since it had up to now been unable to provide an adequate basis for planning

Soviet educationists are now in a position to develop such a system of concepts as a block on which to build an integrated theory of educational content, a theory oriented towards educational practice. It is this system of concepts that the present book purports to explore.

2. TOWARDS A THEORY OF CONTENT
FOR GENERAL SECONDARY EDUCATION

Definition and explanation for a specific purpose would be inadequate unless they were carried out with method. Thanks to modern progress, it is now possible to adopt an approach taking into account modern science in general and scientific methodology in particular. Whereas in the last century a researcher only needed to substantiate results that were already obtained, today all research projects can and should be substantiated theoretically before they are actually launched. It has become normal practice to devise the methodology beforehand. On the contrary, a retrospective description of the stages of discovery justifying what has already happened can no longer remain the predominant, let alone unique, form for explaining an emergent science[4].

A methodology developed on the basis of the entire body of available data greatly facilitates the emergence and constructive development of new branches of science. It enables the 'gestation' period of an emergent science to be reduced and the diminution of trial-and-error methods which involve so much waste of time and duplication of effort.

Methodology can be viewed as having four levels: (a) *philosophical methodology*, i.e. that part of philosophy which is concerned with methodology; (b) *methodological principles common to all sciences* and all kinds of research; (c) the *methodology of a particular science*, i.e. the sum-total of approaches, methods and principles of research pertaining to a particular science (e.g. biology, educational science, etc.); (d) the *methods and techniques of a particular piece of research*[5]. Having accepted the differentiation of methodology into levels for the purpose of developing a theory of curriculum content, one is free to rely upon similar experience in other sciences for establishing methodologies to develop theories.

Thus, the development of theory should follow the pattern prescribed by these four levels. It should pursue a definite goal to the exclusion of a purely intuitive, random search for various concepts that are likely to yield a theory. It is time to subordinate all the empirical data available to the single purpose of developing an integrated teaching theory of general education. The development of this theory depends on the availability of an adequate methodological basis and an adequately analysed body of empirical data.

Crucial to the formulation of a theory are the primary criteria derived from philosophy. This elevated perspective is always applicable, especially when an attempt is being made to put forward a theory, since a theory by definition is based on philosophical premises rather than experimental data[6]. The most important criterion at the philosophical level, which will determine both the content of Soviet formal education and the theory underlying it, is the all-round development of the personality, understood as intellectual, moral, aesthetic and physical self-fulfilment. Marx, Engels and Lenin regarded this as a vital objective of human society. Proclaiming that 'every man enjoys an absolute right to complete self-fulfilment', Engels believed that 'a society organized on communist principles will grant its members an opportunity to apply all their abilities'[7].

In terms of a theory of curriculum content, this formula should be interpreted as having more than one aspect to it. Thus, from the sociological viewpoint, it may be regarded as a comment upon education's role in socialization. Indeed, as a social institution, education is called upon to satisfy: the existing demand of the productive sector for trained manpower; the existing demand among the population (groups or individuals) for education, i.e. for the development of its members' personal abilities; the existing demand in society for the reproduction of its own social structure, and for its members to attain all-round development, which would tend to make this structure more homogeneous. In the broadest possible sense, education can be defined as a means to preserve and develop culture.

Secondly, curriculum content determines the attainment of such aims as: imparting to the pupils reliable and informative knowledge; teaching them to deepen that knowledge by themselves and to use it; encouraging a communist outlook and morals; improving the pupils' health — providing physical training; preparing them for useful work and to participate in the social life of society; making them aware of the necessity to choose the vocation in which they are likely to perform best; helping them to attain the harmony of thought, emotion and intention. All of these aims are but components of the goal of comprehensive and harmonious development of the personality.

Thirdly, there is the social participation aspect of curriculum content. Comprehensive personality development is not confined to a strictly professional activity, but assumes personal enrichment and socialization on as broad a scale as possible, which means a whole system of activities, social contacts and a wide variety of interests.

A mature personality depends above all on the existence of an integrated social structure in which a person can flourish and where individual 'imbalance' and 'incompleteness', which are a consequence of the social division of labour, do not exist. A mature personality, and the interlinkage of its qualities, manifest themselves in the sphere of social activities and relations. It is incumbent upon an education system to get young people involved in a sector of social participation.

In the fourth place, curriculum content has a psychological aspect to it that includes the structural elements of personality — elements to be moulded through the process of education.

And finally, there is an integral educational aspect. As educationists we are, above all, concerned with this ultimate aspect. Indeed, it is from the vantage of the educational sciences that one is able to scan the entire domain of education, i.e. all that is taught and learned, and how it is taught and learned. To enable such an overview, one at first approaches all this complexity from different angles but, in the final analysis, it is the educational sciences, with their particular functions and objectives, that should give an overall perspective.

The concept of unity between theory and practice is another major criterion at the philosophical level on which to base curriculum content. This unity derives from a principle of dialectical materialism: practice determines the functioning and development of understanding, man's practical and creative activities being impossible if they do not reflect the laws governing reality.

Indeed, through his powers of reasoning, man is able to forestall the actual course of events, i.e. on the basis of what exists, he can imagine the possibilities of what is going to happen, thus being in a position to transform reality according to his actual needs[8].

In terms of theory, the general basis for the forecasting of educational reality is exemplified in a principle that man perceives reality not only as it is at a given moment, but also as what it ought to be to satisfy his social needs. Understanding creates images of not only what exists but also of what should exist: '...the world does not satisfy man and man decides to change it by his activity'[9]. It is incumbent on the educational sciences to substantiate and develop theoretical concepts, since nothing but a theory can provide a basis for a large-scale reform as long as it reveals key elements of subject area and explains the phenomena therein[10]. According to Simonjan, who has written on the philosophy of unity between theory and practice, 'theory actually influences practice, otherwise it would be of no significance whatever. This role of theory demonstrates its unity with practice.'[11]. This statement is fully applicable to the educational sciences or, let us say, particularly applicable.

The educational sciences are thus expected to predict and transform, to look beyond what the teachers and educators are capable of seeing in their day-to-day work. To be able to do so, the educational sciences have to draw upon the entire human cultural heritage, human social practice, the entire human social experience (including the way this experience is recorded).

First of all, educationists have to weigh up carefully the actual possibilities and procedures of practical educational activity. There are many other things they have to take into consideration, such as the entire body of educational experience accumulated over centuries past. They have to rely upon the data of philosophy, since educational theory, like other theories, has immediate connections with philosophical knowledge and concepts. Next, educationists have to acquire basic knowledge on the development of theory and the methods of scientific research in general. The most important element of that methodology is exemplified in the philosophical guidelines. Other and more concrete guidelines (of the second, scientific level) are exemplified in the logic and methodology of science, and special studies in the field of education aimed at: identifying trends in the educational sciences as a whole and in their sub-divisions; clarifying the links between the sub-divisions of the educational sciences and the connections with other sciences; revealing how the educational sciences and practice are interconnected; reflecting the composition, function and structure of educational theory underlying educational practice; establishing educational terminology, etc. The educational sciences cannot function without knowledge of sociology, psychology and physiology, neither can they function without knowledge of the content and logic of the subjects underlying education and instruction, as far as the corresponding school subjects are concerned.

This cataloguing of sources of scientific knowledge contributing to the educational sciences and enabling them to guide the teachers does not end there. It is simply not possible to make an exhaustive inventory of all the applications to the educational sciences of knowledge and methods of existing and emerging sciences, not to mention those likely to emerge and become of value to education in the future.

What makes all the difference in this particular case is that we are dealing with a sum total of social experience in its educationally processed and conceptualized form, rather than with the data of educational practice alone. It is the findings of educational research in addition to educational practice that provide further insights. The educational sciences are assigned an active role in education instead of providing a mirror-like image of work already performed.

After this overview of the application of the educational sciences from the vantage of the unity between theory and practice, it is possible to describe in more concrete terms — at the level of a particular science — how this unity manifests itself in the substantiation of teaching (by definition incorporating curriculum content).

Identified at the stage of scientific substantiation are a number of transitions from one component to the next. The most important is the transition from science to practice, i.e. from theoretical reflexions on educational systems towards standardized educational activity laid down in syllabuses, curricula, textbooks and recommendations, all of which may be described in general terms as an educational blueprint (a transition 'from factual components to value judgements' in the words of Hirst[12]).

In analysing this transition in still greater detail[13], we tried to imagine it as a sequence of intellectual reasoning: (a) from a theoretical model of instruction representing the idea of current educational practice towards a normative model representing the general idea of what should exist, i.e. what the content and process of teaching should be and how one should update and transform them; (b) from a normative model towards an instructional blueprint presenting this latter model in terms of actual activity — both models remaining part of educational theory in the broader sense.

The theoretical model is made up of the following stages: (1) definition of the educational system using all the concepts available; (2) a description of teaching at the empirical level in terms of the educational sciences and also in terms of psychology, cybernetics and any other sciences which have a bearing on instruction; (3) on this basis, the educational elements of instruction are assembled into a theory, i.e. by reducing the multiple empirical phenomena to a theoretical entity.

Having constructed a theoretical model, this function of the educational sciences is followed by its normative function. Soviet educationists have always maintained that it is not possible to reduce the educational sciences either to pure theorising or pure practice. Indeed, the educational sciences not only describe and explain educational phenomena, but also govern teaching and upbringing, these two aspects being closely interconnected.

The transition from the theoretical function to the normative function is made possible by way of repeated analyses of reality, this time from the position of the theoretical knowledge already acquired and for the purpose of consolidating that knowledge. The next stage is the transition to a normative model proper, a blueprint for activity, the practical application of a theory.

Even though much simplified, Figure 1 presents the main stages of the above process, this presentation also serving to illustrate one aspect of the unity between theory and practice as manifested in our particular field.

Content building at the level of syllabuses and textbooks, i.e. at the blueprint level, is guided by normative knowledge. At least to some extent, this knowledge is a useful component serving as a foundation for the content of secondary education. Examining curriculum content at the normative level involves deriving from theoretical concepts guidelines of a general and particular nature concerning curriculum content as it will finally appear in syllabuses and textbooks.

FIGURE 1. Towards an educational blueprint.

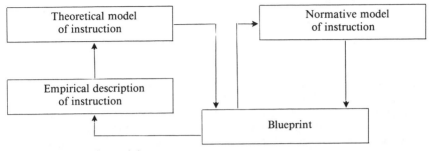

At every stage of the process presented in Figure 1, it appears necessary to verify the conclusions put forward at the research stage. The final results of curriculum construction can be evaluated only when the blueprint has been put into practice, i.e. syllabuses and textbooks. It is at the stage of putting content into practice in educational situations that the final 'empirical' touches are applied to the blueprint, and hence the theory underlying it. Accordingly, on the diagram this kind of feedback is presented in a very general form as an arrow running along the bottom and indicating the implementation of the blueprint in practice.

The goals of education, manifesting themselves in the blueprint of its content, have yet to be defined and introduced, as it were, on the classroom floor. It is essential in developing a theory to have regard for its introduction. According to Lenin, practice is 'higher than (theoretical) knowledge, for it has not only the merit of universality, but also of immediate actuality'[14]

To analyse curriculum content from this stance is to examine it first and foremost as teacher/pupil interaction in the process of instruction. It is only possible to examine curriculum content apart from teaching as such in abstract, restricted terms. In practical, realistic terms, education is an inseparable whole in which teaching and learning, content and process exist side by side.

The content and process of education influence each other in two areas.

The first is that of the *educational situation*. In real terms, educational content exists in the situation of teacher/pupil interaction. It is distributed over the stages and forms of education. Portions of curriculum content are dealt with (imparted by teachers and learned by pupils) at every lesson. Curricula manifest themselves in educational situations as the content component of teaching combined with the process component of teaching.

The second area is that of *reflection*. For the purposes of analysis and construction, curriculum content may be examined in this case in isolation from educational activity. In this form, it can 'exist' in curriculum, but not in reality.

Whenever these two areas are not differentiated, the separation of content from process that can only be imagined in one's mind is taken to exist in reality. Then, the educational situation may be said to be torn asunder. Each of the two fragments in such a case is substantiated individually and the sole remaining basis upon which to select educational content is the logic and data of the science, the elements of which are taught in school.

The history of the educational sciences and practice shows that attempts at developing instructional methods and material, without taking into consideration educational factors and research findings, have invariably proved futile.

Thus, educational periodicals in the United States dwelt some years ago upon the inadequacy of twelve high school textbooks authored by eminent mathematicians and published in the 1958-66 period. The publications originated from a study conducted by panels of experts as part of a nationwide educational reform. Summing up criticisms levelled at the panels, Kline[15], discloses that their recommendations were chiefly those of university professors seated on the panels and exclusively guided by the logic and latest developments in their science. The resultant syllabuses and textbooks received much unfavourable comment and in the end had to be revised. Most of the criticisms stressed the need for thorough educational evaluation. It was also stressed that, while the preceding syllabuses failed to provide proper motivation for the study of mathematics, the newly compiled ones furnished no motivation at all. In the critics' opinion, the compilers would have done well to open the students' eyes to the fact that mathematics was a science that helps man to understand and utilize natural phenomena. Pointing out the link between mathematics and the natural sciences would have made the concepts and theorems more lifelike and may have convinced the students of the significance of mathematics in various applied fields. The critics also regretted the fact that the new syllabuses and textbooks directed the students to go into the deeper intricacies of logic, which had only resulted in the students falling back on the rote learning of mathematics in the spirit of the abolished syllabuses. None of the panels assigned to develop new syllabuses seems to have thought of starting by trying to define the goals of either primary or secondary education. According to Kline, a major blunder of the mathematics professors compiling the syllabuses was a disregard of proper educational factors. Oblivious of the fact that normally it takes years to master mathematics, the textbook revisers had concluded that they could make the young brains do the trick in less time. The professors concentrated on the deductive character of structures which they themselves had had no difficulty mastering, instead of on the prospects for developing mathematical reasoning in the pupils.

One may be reminded in this connection of the criticism levelled by New York teachers at a foreign language syllabus prepared in the early 1960s, which was based on an audiolingual method. Following their criticism that syllabus too was revised. The New York teachers had simply 'demolished' the draft on the grounds that it was detached from educational reality. Some of their objections were: it took too much study time to comply with all the provisions in the syllabus; a foreign language cannot be taught without resort to the mother tongue — the teachers had to give the meaning of words and explain the grammar in the mother tongue even though the syllabus discouraged it; grammar cannot be dispensed with, the simple repetition of pattern phrases failed to satisfy intellectually advanced students who needed logical explanation[16]. Here one is dealing with an obvious collision between projected content and an educational situation, no matter how reliable the scientific foundation for that content may be. The substantiation of teaching solely on a content basis of the science to be taught is increasingly appreciated by curriculum planners and textbook authors as inadequate.

Thus, the content of geography in school should be regarded not merely as a summary of content of the science of geography, but also as something owing its origins to the educational sciences as well.

The function of the educational sciences, as far as the content of general education is concerned, is that of giving a blueprint on which (in modern conditions) educational content should be constructed. It is also incumbent on these sciences to indicate the subject content on which to base educational content. Thus, in the particular case of geography, such an approach can be formulated by answering the following questions: (1) How much curriculum content should there be in the school geography course? (2) How should the school geography course satisfy the requirements of general education? (3) How to draw up a school course of geography to ensure the attainment of general education goals? (4) What theoretical and factual knowledge, intellectual procedures and practical skills are to be acquired in the school geography course compared with the goals and content of general education?

It is obviously insufficient to rely solely on geography to pinpoint the correct answers. These can be identified only in terms of both education and science, which means considering such factors as the goals and content of general education, the principles of teaching, the teaching process for each subject, the specific conditions under which this process takes place, the best forms to be used in the teaching process to present each lesson, i.e. the methods and organizational forms of teaching. Of course, one could simply rely on the consensus of opinion of educationists and geography scholars. Yet, it appears more appropriate to make a special study to identify what general education aspects the school subject of geography is related with, in what way can this subject serve the objectives of general education, and which parts of the geography syllabus best correspond to the goals of general education. In short, it is by inquiring into the educational situation as a whole that one is most likely to find out how this reality can be transformed and improved.

As we have already said, curriculum planners are aware of the inadequacy of basing instruction solely on the basis of the subject without taking into consideration the potential of the pupil and the actual conditions of the teaching process. However, miscalculations may still be possible. The mathematics syllabuses and textbooks which were approved for use in the Soviet school in the 1970s are just a case in point. Practical experience in using these materials for teaching shows them neither to serve the goals of general secondary education effectively nor to measure up with the classroom situation. Concern has been voiced in the press over this fact and it was pointed out that the syllabuses and textbooks proposed by a panel of experts for the study of mathematics in school had been adopted somewhat hastily for use without being properly evaluated in terms of methodology and the educational sciences. Basic facts and essential skills in these instructional materials were overshadowed by a multitude of side-issues susceptible to a multitude of interpretations. It is incumbent on the school to teach the pupil to think, to stimulate intellectual development, and to encourage the pupil to use his brains actively. An approach which lacks such dynamic elements is exemplified by certain instructional materials that have managed to find their way into the mathematics syllabuses. In the circumstances, one cannot but be encouraged by the press campaign in favour of mathematics instruction based on scientific, educational and psychological premises.

In contemplating how a theory of curriculum content could best be developed we took note of the fact that the current findings of educational research were sufficient to provide a broad but purely educational basis. A new evaluation is needed that would take fuller account of the optimum way to teach and of many other purely educational factors. This applies equally to the construction of curriculum content in general and the compilation of the content for particular school subjects.

Be that as it may, a truly scientific justification of the content of a particular school subject is not reducible to an assessment of the subject based solely on the interests of the science to be taught.

As for the optimum way teaching processes should be conducted, it is enough to look back in the history of education to see that ever since psychology grew out of philosophy as a science in its own right, its data have been employed in substantiating this particular aspect of education (including its socialization component). It appears to be appropriate to dwell at some length on the psychological substantiation of educational practice, since it is psychology that, both by tradition and its very nature, has invariably been the instrument of education.

The educational sciences emerged at a time when the traditional sciences, including philosophy, were being differentiated into more specialized fields. Since their inception, the educational sciences have been almost solely concerned with a psychological substantiation of educational concepts (Pestalozzi, Herbart). The role of psychology in education increased as psychology gained ground as a science. And no wonder. While imparting knowledge to any human being (in the school situation, to a child), the teacher simply cannot do without developmental psychology. It stands to reason that any teacher needs to know the psychology of his pupil, the patterns of his intellectual development, in order to be able to teach effectively. Until the educational sciences had collected data enough to justify the name of a discipline, the theoretical substantiation of teaching had typically been the virtual monopoly of psychology. This was not merely expedient but indeed essential; just as, typically, outstanding educationists of the past were philosophers and psychologists first and educationists second.

Today, the situation has altered. The educational sciences are now past their infancy and, besides, didactics — a purely educational theory of teaching — has already delimited its own research domain. Psychology has lost its tutelage of teaching practice. To influence educational practice directly, psychological knowledge has now to be, as it were, filtered through the entire body of evidence of the educational sciences in which interest focuses on the socialization of the young. It is only the entire sciences of education, concentrating on a specific sector of social life, that are able, with due adequacy and immediacy, to take care of practice.

There is a difference in principle between the trend in methodology known as 'psychologism', according to which psychology is the only basis of educational practice, and another view according to which psychology is no more than a specialized discipline even though it has always been a major source for justifying teaching and upbringing.

Psychologism has invariably found its devotees among educationists. Thus, Claparède believed that the educational sciences should be wholly based on developmental psychology and hence the proper role of psychology was that of a theory underlying educational practice. Dewey wrote in his *Psychology and social practice* that psychological theory should lead and enlighten practice; in his view, psychology was a working hypothesis, while education was an experimental verification and illustration of that hypothesis[17]. He suggested setting up a triumvirate of a psychologist/theorist, an educational conceptualist and a teacher/practitioner[18]. The conceptualist was to play the role of a mediator between psychological theory and educational practice. This view was shared by James who asserted that psychology was a science while teaching was an art, and that to pass from science to teaching one needed a mediator to translate the findings of psychology into practical terms[19].

Such concepts cannot be dismissed as belonging to the past; they still survive owing to the confusion of two sciences, the object of study of educational research being equated with the object of the teacher's activity, i.e. with the child's mentality (or that of any other person taught). It is claimed that the educational sciences and instructional practice have the same object of study — a child. This is far from being the case. The object of study (and also the means and results) of science and practice should not be conceived as identical. Already in 1922, Makarenko came up with this unequivocal formulation that the object of study of the educational sciences is specific to that science: 'The prevailing view today is to consider a child as the object of study for educational research. To my mind this is not correct. The true object of educational research is an educational phenomenon'[20]. This is not to remove a child from the field of interest of educational research. Educational research itself has for its object of study neither a child nor an adult (their mentalities being the object of study of psychology), but rather a system of educational activity (the educational situation and associated phenomena). Presented in greater detail, the object of study of educational research includes pupil/teacher interaction, methods of teaching and upbringing, the organization and content of education, the ways in which that content is included into the educational process, etc.

To ignore all this in the belief that the object of study for psychology (in this particular instance, the matters pertaining to one's inner world) is the same as the object of study of the educational sciences would amount to limiting the latter's content to applying psychological findings to construct a system of practical educational measures. Since the object of study of the educational sciences in such a narrow view is fully covered by the objective of psychology, the very category of knowledge of the educational sciences becomes superfluous.

Neither can one readily accept the view (often implied if not expressed) that psychology should be given an absolute prerogative to lay down the rules and norms for the educational practitioner to follow. The acceptance of such a view would inevitably result in an overlapping of functions. Indeed, besides psychology, the educational sciences draw upon many other sources in establishing norms for educational activity.

A restrictive definition of the domain of the educational sciences and an unrestrictive definition of the domain of psychology are likely to give rise to attempts at deriving educational norms exclusively from psychological bases, e.g. teaching principles from learning practices. This approach amounts to ignoring the aims and content of general education, the teacher's activity, the conditions and possibilities of the education/socialization process and a host of other educational factors. Thus, in methodology manuals one comes across assertions that the practices of language acquisition should serve as a natural basis for language learning at school and that even principles of methodology from which teaching standards derive should likewise derive from these practices. Such sweeping derivations obviously lack consistency. Sooner or later, the researcher becomes aware that logic is not solely relevant in drawing a connection between regularity and principle; to do this one has to go beyond pure logic and study the facts arising in the real-life process of teaching an actual subject. And this is only too natural, since education is a unity of two types of activity: teaching (the teacher's activity) and learning (the pupil's activity) and, no matter how hard one may study any of the types (learning in this case), no logic will be enough to derive principles that would effectively govern education as a whole. Attempts at deriving educational norms (principles, recommendations or guidelines) solely from the data of psychology prove, as a rule, untenable. Let us refer, by way of example, to the practical experience of non-translation methods of language teaching at school since there is a vast body of reliable evidence available on that subject.

These methods are based on a psychological postulate that, once one has begun thinking in a foreign language without having to resort to the mother tongue, one is already in perfect command of the language. This prompted a conclusion that, from the beginning, the mother tongue should be excluded from the process of teaching, which, by the way, has never been proved possible in actual practice. Later on, such lop-sided ways of substantiating methods mainly from the viewpoint of linguistics and psychology led to the disregard of educational realities (real classroom settings during a lesson) and to the social demands placed on language teaching, being ignored, i.e. the very demands which these methods were expected to be instrumental in satisfying.

This is not to deny the relevance of psychology in developing the principles of teaching. Yet, even though the knowledge of psychological practices (not necessarily to the exclusion of other forms of knowledge) is obviously essential, it is by no means the only source to rely upon in developing general principles of and particular recommendations for the adequate organization of educational activity. The real question is not whether the educationist needs to know about psychology, but where, how and why it is to be applied. A psychological study may help towards identifying why there is a disparity in a particular case between the 'ideal' lesson and the way things really are on the classroom floor. And then again, it may be relevant to study the psychology of a cohort of pupils in order to come up with concrete recommendations to the teacher. A similar study may be relevant on many other occasions as, for example, in measuring the degree to which instructional material is made use of in the actual process of teaching. Whatever the setting or level of education may be, the primary consideration for educationists remains the educational theory behind the entire system of teaching/learning relationships and factors characteristic of a given educational situation.

Since the data of psychology relating to personality structure are obviously useful in analysing the mechanisms of the psychological activity to be developed in every pupil, a description of educational aims, and hence curriculum content, in terms of psychology may likewise prove useful. Thus, Handschin, a United States educationist, divided the educational aims for a particular school subject (a foreign language) into two groups. Under the first heading he grouped such aims as learning to speak and read the language and becoming familiar with the culture of the country where the language is spoken; leaving under the other heading an aim generated by educational psychology: the acquisition of certain psycho-intellectual qualities. According to Handschin, these qualities are proficiency, discipline, erudition and intellectual enjoyment[21].

It appears quite legitimate to define educational aims in terms of psychology. Yet, in selecting 'psychological aims' one should be guided by the aims of general education, i.e. social aims are determinant. Indeed, it would be more appropriate in this case to refer not to psychological aims, but to the psychological characterization of social aims or a psychological expression of social goals.

It is just as inappropriate to reduce the scientific evaluation of curriculum content to a mere conformity of instructional material with the present-day level of a particular science as it is inappropriate to try to substantiate teaching principles and methods solely on the basis of psychological concepts. This inappropriateness becomes quite plain the moment curriculum content which has been substantiated in this manner comes into conflict with the educational situation in which it is being imparted to the pupils.

Neither is it appropriate to involve a greater number of sciences in constructing curriculum content, since each of the sciences has for its subject only part of education — and not the whole of it. It stands to reason that for an adequate development of curriculum content, one needs a scientific discipline that would permit a unified approach to the selection of both the content and method of instruction. Given this, it should be possible to substantiate curriculum content as a component of educational activity to be linked with its process component. It is incumbent upon *didactics*, an educational discipline now being developed by Soviet educationists, to serve as an educational theory of instruction. The following section describes a didactic approach to constructing a theory of content for general secondary education.

3. DIDACTICAL APPROACH TO A THEORY OF CURRICULUM CONTENT

We propose the following definition of didactics as a theory of instruction in its present state of development: *didactics is the educational science concerned with instruction and the curriculum content imparted through teaching.* In the development of the educational sciences as a whole, didactics is gaining ever greater independence as a discipline with its own particular domain of research which differs from the research domains of other educational disciplines and related sciences. At the same time, the definition of the domain of didactics poses a challenging problem to the methodologists of the educational sciences.

Fundamental to defining this domain is the principle of unity between theory and practice. As with the educational sciences in their entirety, didactics is concerned with practice and specifically with educational activity. Besides reflecting educational practice, it is incumbent upon didactics to influence that practice, thus serving the teacher an instrument to transform and improve it. In order to expedite the advancement of practice, didactics has to provide a scientific foundation for educational practice, which is its main function. This function is absolutely essential in defining the domain of didactics.

Another principle of general methodology to be used as a guide in defining the domain of didactics is that man's intellectual power is active by nature. Indeed, understanding cannot be reduced to contemplation, to a 'photographic' reproduction of reality. Reality is comprehended through man's sensual activity — practice[22].

We share with philosophers specializing in the methodology of science the differentiation between 'the general object of study of science' and 'the particular object of study of science'. The general object of study is that part of reality with which the researcher is concerned, while the particular object of study is that part of the general object with which the researcher is concerned as a representative of a particular science.

Researchers representing particular sciences tend to view the same object differently since each science has its own goals and its own system of concepts and it is only too natural for each specialist to stress particular aspects, relationships and interactions as far as the given general object is concerned. Thus, teaching may be studied by an educationist, methodologist, psychologist and cyberneticist. Yet, each of them is likely to identify that which falls within his particular province of interest, and to set particular aims for that interest, which presupposes formulation of these aims and presentation of the results in terms of a particular science. All the above specialists may decide to attend the same lesson as observers. They will see the same things happen, but each will focus on what is most relevant for his particular discipline. The educationist will probably keep an eye on the way the teacher applies general teaching methods and the principles underlying these methods. The methodologist specializing in the subject taught at the lesson will, in all likelihood, concentrate on the conformity of teaching methods and the content of instructional material with the aims which have been established for the teaching of that subject at school. The psychologist will be more interested in the manifestation of known patterns of acquisition of instructional material in the school matrix, while the cyberneticist will see in the lesson such inevitable characteristics of a control system as rapport and feedback.

The distinction between the general and particular objects of study of a science is essential both in theory and practice. It enables priorities to be established, especially when a comprehensive and meaningful study is contemplated with a view to taking decisions which are likely, just as meaningfully, to influence follow-up action. And this distinction becomes simply crucial if and when interest is focused on human activity and specifically on educational activity.

The definition of a particular object of study of didactics cannot be reduced, as is generally the case, to its field of research (including the fields of research of related sciences) if we really intend to progress beyond the delineation of a general object of didactic research to tackling its particular object of study. A comprehensive definition of the latter means that its components should be presented as a whole unit so as to assume their real significance in a system of didactic concepts. To come up with such a definition, one has to examine teaching from a particular angle, which means drawing on the whole body of data on instruction collected by the educational sciences in order to determine the level which didactics is to attain to keep pace with scientific progress, the functions and prospects of didactics and, what is most important, the degree to which didactics should substantiate practical instruction, i.e. teachers' practical activity. If such a definition of the particular object of didactics were available, the research in this field would not only enrich the educational sciences but indeed help the educationists to organize educational practice correctly. A particular object of study for didactics can be better understood by answering the following questions: in the current situation, in what way should instruction be presented as the object of study of didactics? Has didactics gained enough scientific experience to reflect educational phenomena adequately? How should didactics reflect its general object (instruction) by drawing upon contemporary definitions in order to furnish scientific justification for educational practice? In short, it appears impossible to define a particular objective of didactics without due regard for its functions, general objective and intellectual procedures. The analysis of these functions and procedures should be conducive to finding appropriate answers to the above questions.

Progress in the educational sciences and in actual practice has brought about profound changes in teaching and the methods of analysing it.

The concept 'instruction' is susceptible of multiple definitions. Such a large part of man's social activity is covered by this concept that not only writers on education but also philosophers, sociologists and psychologists are awaiting its exhaustive definition. In abstract terms, the faculty of learning is typical of all living systems. In terms of cybernetics, instruction is understood even more broadly to the point of assuming the existence of self-instructional systems. However, in terms of the educational sciences, which form part of the social sciences, instruction is regarded as an exclusively social phenomenon. In educational terms, it is a means to transfer social experience. It is first and foremost an integral part of human activity.

The instructional process is commonly described as the sum-total of a sequence of teacher/pupil interactions for the sole purpose of transferring knowledge, skills and desirable behaviour. This description is somewhat superficial, the above interactions occurring in a context visible, as it were, to the naked eye. Yet, the essence of teaching is something more than meets the eye. In terms of didactics, a point of departure in revealing this essence is on the social plane. Indeed, in analysing instructional phenomena, this plane is of primary importance.

The strategy for revealing the essence may be summarized as follows: what happens in the classroom is understood to have repercussions far beyond the classroom walls. The readily visible sequence of interactions of individuals participating in the instructional process is connected in the analyst's mind with social activity in its universal sense. Given all this, these interactions will be seen as no more than concrete manifestations of a much broader process of instruction as a social activity. Instruction is not reducible to an arithmetic total of actions by the teacher and by the pupils, treated as just so many individuals.

In constructing an educational theory much will depend on how educational activity and the human subjects involved in it are viewed in terms of that theory. A distinction must be drawn between 'individual subject' and 'collective or social subject'. The very existence of social subjects becomes possible owing to the existence of a programme for a multitude of individuals. Such multitudes are groups of people whose actions are so co-ordinated as to comprise a system with specific patterns of behaviour not reducible to the actions of any individual in the group[23].

The next step in discovering the essence of the instructional process thus involves not merely two individuals — one of whom teaches and other learns — but rather social subjects, i.e. all those who either teach or learn under an approved common programme of activity which has been compiled by educational bodies at various levels working in co-ordination, a programme which we designate 'a blueprint for instruction'. Such a blueprint, once it has assumed the form of syllabuses, textbooks, guidelines, lesson-plans, sets of visual aids, etc., becomes an important element in the process of teaching — a social phenomenon. Where mass compulsory education exists, the introduction of such blueprints in the form of 'core curricula' becomes inevitable, even in countries with a decentralized education system. In a lecture at the University of London in June 1982 on a core curriculum for the general education school, Skilbeck described it as '... that part of the whole curriculum which in broad outline is common to all schools, defined in partnership by central and local bodies and interpreted by schools (based on analyses of contemporary culture)'. The need for a core curriculum is justified, for instance, in the documents of the Department of Education and Science (United Kingdom). In one of them, dated 1977, it is interpreted by the schools' inspectorate as 'a body of skills, concepts, attitudes and knowledge, to be pursued, to a depth appropriate to their ability, by all pupils in the compulsory years of secondary education for a substantial part of their time, perhaps as much as two-thirds or three-quarters of the total time available'[24].

Another working paper of the Department of Education and Science stresses the need for a 'nationally agreed framework for the curriculum'[25]. A third working paper, dated 1981, touches upon the need to join the forces of public educators to 'secure a school curriculum which measures up to the whole range of national needs and also takes account of the range of local needs'[26].

Hirst defines curriculum in more detail as:

...a programme of activities (by teachers and pupils) designed so that pupils will attain as far as possible certain educational aims or objectives... in curriculum decisions we are concerned with a programme of intentional, deliberate and consciously planned activities... these activities are planned so that certain objectives will be reached, so that the pupils will come to know certain things, have certain skills, will be able to appreciate certain things, have certain habits, patterns of emotional response and so on... curriculum activities are planned as the means whereby these objectives are reached[27].

Furthermore, Hirst stresses the need to establish 'institutions which deliberately plan programmes of activities to bring about pupils' learning'[28].

Thus, there is an obvious tendency to single out the substantiation and development of materials underlying the planned conduct of teaching — instructional blueprints — as a branch of activity in its own right. Today, teaching is no longer a field in which any teacher has a carte blanche, but a sector in which they exercise their profession in partnership and are guided by a programme developed likewise in partnership.

In educational literature there are numerous signs of increasing appreciation of the social significance of teaching and the consequences deriving from this fact for the construction of an educational theory. Thus, Beardsley maintains:

Instruction may be improvised or it may be thought out (at least in its main strategic outlines) in advance. Such an advance plan or design for an educational experience or a sequence of educational experiences is (if I may be permitted a somewhat tainted contemporary term) an educational scenario, which might be drawn up as a textbook or a syllabus or a 'unit-plan'. Finally, the theory of teaching (which I take to be at least a substantial part of what is often called 'educational theory') consists of general principles — both normative and non-normative — for constructing educational scenarios of various sorts for various kinds of persons. Since its non-normative principles are general facts about human beings, the theory of instruction is ...an applied social science[29].

It would be exaggeration, in our opinion, to equate the educational theory of instruction with an applied social science. Yet, it would be quite fair to connect the social nature of educational activity to its 'scenario'.

The integrity of instruction, so far as its social role is concerned, finds expression in the concept of unity of teaching and learning as an interaction between individuals performing teaching and learning functions. As a result, an approach to a number of seemingly habitual notions and phenomena is in many aspects completely altered. Thus, one of the components of the above unity (learning) may now be defined in educational terms as an activity being performed by a collective subject — a multitude of people — acquiring social experience as it is understood by educationists, i.e. curriculum content.

The distinction between this didactic interpretation of teaching and its psychological interpretation becomes increasingly obvious as one turns to psychological data available in literature. Abulhanova believes an 'individual' to be a subject of psychical activity and tends to connect the 'problem' to be solved through psychical activity 'with the individual's specific existence, the individual's mode of existence'[30]. Lingart, believing learning to be a specific form of individual activity, remarks that the psychology of learning at present regards its various aspects as a universal phenomenon occurring in the behaviour of complex animate and inanimate systems[31]. At any rate, it may be taken for granted that there is a wide gap between the behaviour of inanimate systems and living man's acquisition of social experience in the educational context.

The view of instruction which we propose to adopt differs in many cardinal aspects from the cybernetics approach which has so far largely served as a basis for programmed instruction, a trend which has lately come into fashion. Those infatuated with programmed instruction recently insisted not merely on the application of certain concepts and terms of cybernetics to didactical analysis but, indeed, on a substitution of cybernetics for educational theory, assuming that cybernetics serves to analyse the general laws of effective control over any process whatever.

Quite a few educationists and psychologists have by now perceived the fallacy of such a substitution. Talyzina, an eminent Soviet educator, remarks:

Teaching and upbringing can very well be described in terms of cybernetics but, firstly, this is not something for the cyberneticists to do for educationists and, secondly, an adequate description of these processes is hardly possible until we know the specific regularities inherent in them[32].

The British scholar O'Connor refers to a 'disappointing development of programmed learning and its application in teaching machines'[33].

To visualize a particular object of study for didactics with greater clarity, one should go beyond considering its general object (instruction in its current state) to consider the status the science of didactics enjoys vis-à-vis other sciences.

Didactics is fast attaining a theoretical status. This process is expedited by the development of science in general and its intellectual potential in particular. Now didactics enters into the state of transition from the empirical (cognition of phenomena) to the theoretical stage (cognition of meaning), a stage sooner or later attained in the process of evolution of a science. In Soviet educational research, increasing recourse is had to such procedures as progression from the concrete to the abstract, modelling, assumption of the ideal, etc. Curriculum content and instructional processes are taken to be a whole in terms of a systems approach. It is by becoming increasingly theoretical that didactics acquires an ever-greater potential to improve and transform educational practice.

Didactics takes a positive view of the unity of teaching and upbringing, since through properly organized teaching the pupils not merely acquire knowledge but also moral attitudes and desirable behaviour.

Neither can one any longer ignore the fact (which we dealt with at some length in the preceding section) that curriculum content exists in the teaching situation. At every stage of this process, no matter how small, there is always present an element of curriculum content. Every minute of the lesson the teacher is imparting and the pupils are acquiring specific pieces of knowledge, definite skills, habits and attitudes; in short, all that comprises curriculum content. The links between and unity of process and content are major characteristics of teaching to be considered in interpreting a particular object of didactics.

And finally, heed should be paid to the fact that instruction has a dual role as regards didactics: as an object of study and as a contribution towards constructing the science of didactics. And this means consciously orienting didactic research on the improvement of instructional practice. Neglecting the practical realities of teaching practice and its characteristics amounts to reducing didactic research to a purely speculative and fruitless exercise. On the other hand, as we have already pointed out in the preceding section devoted to the unity of theory and practice, in the absence of proper theoretical substantiation, didactic recommendations for the improvement of teaching are hardly likely to lead to improvement.

Presented in brief below are the chief characteristics of didactics.

Didactics tends to view instruction, first and foremost, as a branch of social practice, which logically follows from its social role. To expand upon this view, instruction is an activity for the purpose of attaining definite educational goals conforming to social demand, an activity which should measure up to a scientifically substantiated blueprint. Specific to this activity is the interconnectedness of teaching and learning as two complementary socially-oriented components operating in unity. Didactics tends to look upon teaching as being allied with upbringing to form an integral whole, which is also associated with the unity between process and content. It is with a view to transforming and improving educational practice that didactics tends to regard instruction not merely as an object of scientific research but also as an object contributing to designing based on scientific principles.

Basing a comprehensive theory of the content of general education on didactics means that it is designed as: (a) a particular educational theory reflecting its object to perform its fundamental function; and (b) furnishing an answer to the question of how to construct the content of education to perform its applied function.

We propose an approach to designing a theory for the content of general education which is based on a sum-total of the methodological criteria presented earlier in this chapter and which presupposes that content be viewed in the unity of the following aspects: its social essence, the educational affiliation of the content, and the systems activity mode of its examination.

Curriculum content is social in nature, since (together with the instructional process) it serves as the principle medium to convey social experience, as well as an educationally adapted expression of this experience, to the younger generation. An adequate interpretation of curriculum content and an equally adequate selection of the means to convey it via teaching should constitute a stimulus to social, technical and scientific development. On the other hand, a failure to define curriculum content correctly or a slipshod preparation of curricula and textbooks are bound to have negative repercussions not only on education but on society as a whole.

However, it would be altogether erroneous to identify curriculum content either with social goals or the sum-total of social experience. It is incumbent upon educationists to express these goals in terms of the educational sciences, to consolidate them in educational terms. It stands to reason that the sum-total of social experience (meaning all the scientific and other knowledge and skills that people have gained) cannot be imparted to every schoolboy and schoolgirl. The construction of curriculum content falls within the province of the educational sciences, which are expected to translate the goals of education into educational terms, consolidate the abstract notions of what to teach so as to enable the teacher to use this knowledge in his day-to-day work. With this in mind, curriculum content is not a mirror-like image of general goals determined by social demands and by the demand to impart social experience to the pupils. The content of general secondary education should rather be interpreted as an educational concept of the above goals or their educational expression — their educational model.

Curriculum content being an educational category, the social demands placed upon formal education should be interpreted in educational terms. Such an interpretation means bringing the projected curriculum content into agreement with the established patterns of instruction and the means currently available to the teacher to convey this content to the pupils. In short, the configuration of the educational model in this case (interlinkage between various elements of content, their sequence, degree of complexity, presentation, etc.) will depend on the objective nature of the educational situation, i.e. the matrix in which educational activity takes place. At the same time, those forms of activity in which curriculum content is actually made available to the younger generation (methods, organization, forms of teaching) will depend on content. Thus, the content and process components of instruction are conceptualized as a unit and two different phenomena all at the same time.

It is by examining curriculum content ontologically, i.e. in those forms in which it really exists in the matrix of instruction, that one can have a scientifically justified image in which both curriculum content (as an educational package of social goals) and the teaching process (as a means to impart that content) are 'specific logical forms occurring beside each other or one inside the other and not one after the other in linear succession'[34].

It would hardly be appropriate today to tackle a problem of any complexity without resorting to a systems approach. In these terms, curriculum content can also be interpreted as a system. Neither can one overlook the fact that this system functions in a matrix of activity, i.e. curriculum content is imparted by the teacher to the pupils within the matrix of educational activity. And finally, curriculum preparation is not a spontaneous process but a process resulting from the activity of educationists, methodologists and other specialists.

Using a systems approach it is possible to visualize the construction of an educational model stage-by-stage, each of the stages corresponding to a level in the construction of actual curriculum content.

One can begin developing a theoretical idea about curriculum content by assuming that it should borrow everything that is vital from social experience and therefore considered essential for the pupils to acquire. This is the level of *theoretical conceptualization*. Here, curriculum content is explained as a system with a definite composition (elements), structure (internal connections) and a social function to perform (to impart social experience translated in educational terms). At this level, one defines what is necessary and possible to impart to the pupils and identifies each vital element of curriculum content serving a definite purpose. Thus, in terms of Soviet comprehensive school education, the function of content is to serve as a means for the all-round development of the younger generation — a means of preparation for active involvement in social life.

Next comes the level of the *school subject*. Here, a more detailed account is given of individual elements of curriculum content performing specific functions in the context of general education. These specific functions determine the composition and structure of the content of each school subject without concealing their common theoretical basis. The idea of what to teach is taking a more definite shape. Those elements of social experience which are to be acquired by the pupil are singled out. All these elements are detailed not only in research papers concerned with the respective subject, but also in normative documents such as curricula and syllabuses.

However, neither curricula nor syllabuses are the final level of laying down content. This takes place at the level of *study material*. The composition of curriculum content outlined at the first level and specified for particular school subject at the second is now given substance: individual items of knowledge, skills and habits, as well as the means to acquire them (exercise books, work books and manuals intended both for teachers' and pupils' use).

It is at these three levels that the construction of the content of general secondary education takes place, a content which is to assume the role of an educational model of social goals. At first, this content takes the form of a project, something which is still taking shape, existing only as an authorized norm, which has yet to acquire a material structure through the process of actual teaching and thus in the pupils' minds. However, the moment it enters the teaching process, it is no longer something imagined but something tangible. Such are the basic steps of constructing curricula.

This theoretical model of curriculum content in its formative stages is functionally structured. In terms of didactics (a science to study this process), content formation is a dynamic process, i.e. the theoretical image of that content acquires concrete shape at the level of the school subject, to be further consolidated at the level of teaching material. Composition at each level contributes to the same process at each subsequent level.

Even though content formation can be conceived as proceeding from the top down — from theoretical concept to practical teaching — there is also a concomitant feedback (see Figure 1), i.e. once study materials have been tested in practice, they become an object of theoretical scrutiny; the advantages and disadvantages revealed by practice pose new theoretical problems. The solution of these difficulties results in a more exhaustive conceptualization at all levels and hence in an improvement of study materials.

Thus, as an object of didactic analysis, curriculum content may be defined as a multi-level model of the social goals of education which, interms of didactics, represents a content component of instruction. The construction of curricula is taken to be a particular objective of didactic research within general secondary education (involving the solution of both basic and applied problems).

Such a definition of the didactic theory of curriculum content, and of its particular purpose, is derived from the characteristics of didactics as an educational discipline. Didactics is not claimed to actually construct curricula, since this is done at the level of analysing the content and teaching of each particular school subject. Didactics is expected to develop general principles upon which to construct curricula — a theoretical basis. A theory of content of general education should not be confounded with a theory of general education, the latter naturally covering a wider field. This is not to deny didactics the opportunity to use data obtained in this wider field of research. Yet, the narrower field of curriculum content appears much more promising for didactic research. Neither a simple reproduction nor a slight modification of the theory underlying general education as a whole would lead to a radical solution of purely didactic problems. From the very beginning one should examine the content of general education strictly within the limits of its construction so as to focus on the development of principles upon which to consolidate curriculum content for school subjects and on the setting of didactic standards for compiling methodological materials for school subjects (didactic standards for curricula and syllabuses, and for structuring teaching material in curricula and textbooks). This is not to reject the idea of analysing and using any sources of knowledge but rather to concentrate research effort on identifying a purely didactic field of interest.

Neither should a theory of the content of general education be reduced to curriculum theory, at least in the manner that itr has been interpreted so far. Despite the many existing definitions[35], the term 'curriculum' is generally understood as covering not only the syllabuses and content of particular subjects, but also the forms and methods of teaching and the evaluation of results.

Furthermore, apart from material on a particular subject, it also covers the pupil who is being instructed, the learning processes and the teaching means available. It is generally understood that one should draw upon the knowledge of various sciences in evaluating the curriculum, i.e. all that is normative in the educational situation. Yet, no or little effort has been made to develop a purely educational theory of curriculum evaluation. Even where the need for such a purpose-oriented philosophical, psychological and sociological evaluation is recognized, little progress ensues. Thus, in a recent important article on the logic of curriculum development, Hirst, while rejecting the idea of directly drawing upon various (non-educational) disciplines for the sole purpose of providing a basis for curriculum, believes that the only solution is to turn to common sense rather than to any educational theory. Besides, curriculum development, according to this author, should be carried out in elements, i.e. in a fragmentary manner, since he sees 'no reason to believe a unified theory of educational practice is possible when any generalizing theory must of its nature be a partial abstraction from the realities of practice'[36].

The theory of content of education we are proposing is 'of its nature' to a certain extent an abstraction. However, whatever the level of abstraction, the defining characteristics of the educational reality are retained (unity of teaching and learning, of content and process). It is no less significant that in evaluating curriculum (or rather that part of curriculum which embodies content) our theory becomes a study of reality from a didactic stance, i.e. from that of an educational theory.

So far, interest in this discourse has focused on the hierarchy of levels in the system of curriculum content in the process of its formation. The following section will examine curriculum content in terms of systems characteristics, such as composition, function and structure.

The *composition of curriculum content* is an educational interpretation of the goals set by society. Taking this content to be an educational expression of social demands means that there is a need to translate a philosophical category of goal (a form of social demand) into an educational category of compositionas a complex of basic elements of the content.

The *function of curriculum content* acquires specific characteristics at every level. The function of the content of general secondary education in the Soviet school is to mould a comprehensively developed personality. The general theoretical concept deriving from the demands placed on education by society, according to the successive levels, creates a basis and source for the construction of curricula.

The *function of a particular school subject* is determined by the specific problems its teaching is to solve in the process of attaining the general goal of education. Thus the specific problems to be solved by teaching geography are obviously different from those to be solved by teaching a foreign language, and it is precisely these kinds of specifics which determine the function of a particular school subject.

The *function of study materials* is determined by the didactic problems of personality moulding, the solution of which depends on specific items of tangible lesson units imparted to the pupils learning a definite subject.

The *structure of curriculum content* is above all determined by the functions of the elements of that content. It reflects the links between its elements at every level of its construction.

Figure 2 presents a somewhat simplified graphic presentation of projected curriculum content in terms of didactic analysis:

FIGURE 2. Simplified presentation of projected curriculum content

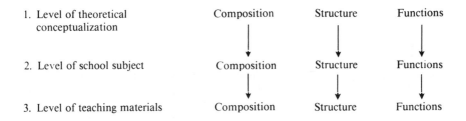

	Composition	Structure	Functions
1. Level of theoretical conceptualization			
2. Level of school subject	Composition	Structure	Functions
3. Level of teaching materials	Composition	Structure	Functions

This is an outline limited to the construction of content at the three levels. Besides analysing the content of general education by levels of construction, it may also be analysed by the characteristics of systems.

4. THEORY OF GENERAL SECONDARY EDUCATION: GOALS AND PROBLEMS

A major feature of the didactic approach to analysing and constructing curriculum content is, as we have already said, the analysis of that content in the context of teaching activity. Thus, the content of education is regarded not as something extraneous to teaching, but in partnership with it, as its own content. From the viewpoint of didactics, curriculum content is examined, as it were, in its context, which is that of education. Such an approach enables the gap between the process and content aspects of education to be overcome, a gap arising firstly when content is constructed as a simple arithmetic total of contents of school subjects without any system, and secondly, when it is constructed without regard to the factors affecting the teaching process, as illustrated by the example in Section 2 earlier in this chapter.

Commonly a gap between projected and resulting content arises when construction has been started at the third level, i.e. at the level of study material for a school subject, or by attempting to develop a curriculum narrowly based on the laws governing a science regardless of didactics, the function of education as such and the role of school subjects.

No amount of subsequent decrease or increase in curriculum content, nor any ensuing attempts to establish inter-subject linkages, can repair the damage, since such an outdated trial-and-error procedure is simply incompatible with modern scientific achievements, let alone the fact that it is ineffective costwise. A more practicable approach is to imagine the composition and structure of curriculum content originating at the theoretical stage, so that it may become more material at every subsequent stage, with the structure of curriculum content gradually becoming clearer as linkages with other school subjects are introduced. This kind of approach should avoid from the very beginning any risk of a gap appearing between the projected content and its subsequent realization, i.e. to mitigate as far as possible the disparities likely to arise between the planned curricula and textbooks on the one hand and the educational context in which they will be used on the other.

The chief aim in evolving a didactic approach to the content of general secondary education is, firstly, to co-ordinate all efforts contributing towards a radical improvement by using a systems approach and by formulating proven criteria so as to satisfy — as far as curriculum content goes — the most exacting demands of society concerning the real possibilities of real schools and real schoolchildren, and, secondly, to make it possible to predict whether the projected content will measure up to these real possibilities. Such an approach to constructing curriculum content using real-life situations enables the elements at different levels to be differentiated. Thus, it should be possible to distinguish between general and specific skills by regarding the latter as a means to realize the former in study materials.

Didactics serves to pinpoint a 'target area' in the general object of study which will be elucidated only through acquiring new knowledge. Thus, one such target area of a specifically didactic nature appears to be the development of and introduction into curriculum content of those 'contracted' models of social activity[37] which should comprise in one system the entire structure of personality being formed in the process of this activity.

In the teaching process, these models have to be 'unfolded' and the activity which is particular to them has to be transmitted by another type of activity (that of teaching), which gives them a specific form distinct from that in which they exist outside the teaching process. Thus, for the purposes of language instruction, educationists have to design an instructional manner of speaking which is different from the manner of speaking to be subsequenytly acquired by the pupils, since teaching situations serve a purpose different from that of natural communication. Teaching situations are artificial by nature, even though the intention is to prepare the pupils to act in real-life settings and not in instructional ones. An instructional problem situation would similarly differ from a problem situation involving cognitive activity by an individual. The former concerns types and forms of teaching activity during a lesson, while the latter is a psychical condition into which the human subject enters whenever he needs new knowledge or to know how to act[38]. Once one examines not merely the pupil's psychical condition but the entire complex of teaching activity, the latter dictates the structural characteristics of situations arising therein. Such situations can be described not only as something already existing but also as something intended as, for example, recommended forms of teaching, recommendations for the teacher to follow, etc. Thus, it should be possible not merely to describe such situations but, indeed, to predict them in advance so as to include them into curriculum content in the form of teaching situations of various types.

So the study of models to 'contract' and 'unfold' activity which will be included into the pattern of specific teaching activity is an objective of purely didactic research. Another aspect of content construction is to give these modes of activity a form that would correspond to the character of teaching activity, making sure that the principle of unity between the content and process of instruction was observed. However, the most important task in this context is to devise a system of instruction (including its content) that would satisfy the demands currently placed on general education by both the social and productive sectors.

A theory underlying the construction of the content of general education is not limited either to the three levels or even the characteristics of systems mentioned above (see section 3). This construction is influenced by a multitude of factors and knowledge, both non-educational and educational: the former include philosophical knowledge; knowledge about the social goals of education; psychological knowledge; subject knowledge (knowledge borrowed from a science taught as a school subject); the latter include knowledge about the teaching process (about teaching methods and the forms of teaching in which the methods are employed, about teaching techniques and settings), knowledge of the principles underlying instruction, etc.

The use of these sources at the different levels of content construction may be presented as follows.

The general theoretical definition of curriculum content begins with the consideration of social demands and the general goals of education based on these demands. The goals are derived from a philosophical analysis and by authors who seek to reveal the sociological aspects of education. The initial conceptualization is based on philosophical methodology, i.e. at the highest level, and subsequently proceeds at the lower levels of methodology.

The need to resort to the second level of methodology — that of principles and research methods common to all sciences — arises as soon as there is need to interpret social goals educationally, to construct an educational model of these goals. At this point there is a need to resort to systems and activity approaches. Analysis serves as a basis for the selection of methods to construct a universal theory of general education, for the ordering and consolidation of curriculum content at different levels, as well as for the identification of the composition, functions and structure of curriculum content as an object of educational research.

Prior to constructing such a theory, it appears important to note that there is a constant increase in the trend towards integrated processes in the field of science. There is a process of synthesis of knowledge for various disciplines which results in an ever-greater significance being attached to purely scientific problems, methods and concepts common to many sciences.

Such ostensibly universal concepts emerging from these processes are descriptive of the characteristics of both existence and cognition. 'System', 'structure', 'element' and 'function' are examples of such concepts. They are typical of any science[39], including didactics. By including the concepts of composition, function and structure in a theory of content of education, we qualify the content as a system and, in terms of didactics, as a systems object. Generalized as it may be, this qualification is helpful in determining the direction in which to proceed in constructing a theory the particular object of which (as that of any theory) should be interpreted as a system of connections[40].

In terms of a didactic theory of curriculum content, such a system means connections of two types: (a) between the composition, structure and function of curriculum content; (b) between the levels of content construction (theoretical conceptualization; school subject; lesson). In this system, curriculum content is in a dynamic state. The first step is an of initial definition, after which a description should be provided of the elements of curriculum content together with their essential connections, the latter being drawn from in didactic theory. In terms of application, there is a need for a normative guideline to indicate how these connections should be established and adapted to consolidate curriculum content into a system such that, from its very inception, it is destined to embody all the necessary elements in the context of educational reality.

Important as it is, familiarization with scientific methodology is still inadequate as a basis for a theoretical overview of curriculum content. For that, it is essential to inquire into the practices and organization of the activity into which curriculum content is included, i.e. teaching. One has to know the structural connections of the instructional process and how the structure of teaching is related to the structure of content at the level of theoretical conceptualization. And finally, as we have already said, there is a need for psychological knowledge in order to have in one's mind a realistic concept of content as part of a global theoretical image.

In selecting sources for constructing curriculum content, one should remember that the process of constructing a school subject is oriented towards the theoretical concept of curriculum content, which must also be regarded as a source.

At the school subject level, the concept of what to teach becomes more specific compared with the preceding level, and those parts of social experience which should be acquired by the pupil are likewise identified with greater clarity. The elements of content composition identified at the first level find expression in the school subject, while the structure is above all determined by the interaction of these elements. On the other hand, each school subject has a specific role to play in the context of general education. Hence both its structure and composition are similarly specific. At the school subject level, one of the sources of construction of curriculum content is a science which is differently reflected in subject content depending on its role in general education. The content of a science, in its educational interpretation, is embodied in the corresponding school subject. This point should be clarified in more detail in view of two major factors.

Firstly, not all school subjects are sciences. For instance, neither foreign language nor literature are sciences. Secondly, even school subjects like physics or history must not be regarded simply as truncated versions of their corresponding sciences.

The introduction of a school subject into the curriculum and the functions of a school subject are determined — as follows from the above — by social demands. If one demand is that pupils should acquire a working knowledge of a foreign language, this does not mean that they are supposed to acquire the fundamentals of linguistics. (This is not to say that language methodologists should not take account of current linguistic data in compiling appropriate manuals and lesson-plans.) Pupils learning a foreign language are only supposed to grasp a few rules of linguistics for purely practical purposes. In this particular case, teaching content should contain no more theory than is helpful in mastering the essential practical skills and habits[41].

Things would be different if the social goal of language study changed and it were recognized that, besides the rudiments of chemistry or biology, those of linguistics should be studied as well. Accordingly, school subject manuals and aids would need to be drastically altered. Instead of the simple conversations, reading exercises and practice drills habitually used in school, textbooks would also include such sections as 'Word and concept', 'Metonymic changes of meanings', 'Literary vocabulary and dialects', etc.

Soviet educationists have recently come up with a theoretically grounded system of foreign-language study paying due heed to the specifically educational role of the subject in attaining the goals of secondary education, to the content and conditions of teaching (the place of language tuition in the curriculum, the number and distribution of teaching hours, the pupils' age, the similarity in type between the language taught and the mother tongue)[42].

The latest attempt at devising a system of language teaching oriented not so much on linguistic or psychological concepts but rather on the real-life settings of actual language use and the corresponding instructional settings is based on the aims of teaching formulated as language functions for the pupil to acquire. The authors seeking to substantiate this system stress that such an approach takes full account of the social context of language use[43] and provides criteria to select language functions and the notions the pupil will have to handle in real-life situations. These criteria include: a general description of the types of language contacts to which the pupil will be exposed as a member of a particular target group; the language activities he will engage in (oral or written, active or passive use of the foreign language); the settings in which he will use the language; the roles (social and psychological) he will play; the topics he will deal with[44].

The subject of literature has for a principal function teaching the pupils to interpret reality through literary works and to increase their artistic appreciation. Scientific knowledge in this context is limited to analysing the essence of literary works in some depth. Literature as a subject has little to do with the logic of a science. The knowledge the pupils acquire in studying this subject cannot be equated with scientific knowledge. The phenomena of reality are portrayed, rather than presented in anything like scientific terms. Even though the pupils may acquire the rudiments of literary criticism, the very designation of literature rather than literary studies pinpoints its real purpose.

Depending on the functions a school subject performs, it is possible to identify the different levels at which it reflects the content of a science.

School subjects corresponding to the natural sciences, such as astronomy, physics, chemistry and biology, as well as to the humanities, such as history and economic geography, typically reflect scientific knowledge. In the matrix of these subjects, science not only serves to explain the phenomena of reality but is indeed an object of study. The pupils become familiar with various scientific theories, come to know how and why they superseded each other in centuries past, how theories develop; they learn methods common to all sciences or to a particular science and, last but not least, how to apply these methods to solving learning problems.

The content of some other subjects may reflect only a few of the concepts of the corresponding sciences. Foreign language, arts subjects and music are just cases in point. Scientific concepts are included into the content of these subjects only as necessary for a conscious mastery of the activity.

The teaching of the mother tongue as a school subject is somewhat specific. Speech development is its primary function and giving the pupils some knowledge linguistics is its secondary one. In the teaching of the mother tongue, science is given the role of a system of knowledge with a function of elucidating various language aspects and subtleties of usage.

And finally, there are a group of school subjects which have an auxiliary role for certain sciences and pursuits (draftsmanship, physical education, manual training, automobile maintenance).

In compiling a school subject, knowledge of the teaching process may prove useful for determining its structure as well as the sequence and scope of its components. The concept of 'school subject', in terms of the unity of content and process, is definable as an entity including, firstly, that part of content which the teacher imparts and the pupil acquires and, secondly, a means whereby the pupil acquires content, develops his intellect and becomes socialized.

Psychological knowledge, in the compilation of a school subject, should be more concrete than that needed in developing a theoretical concept of curriculum content. It is more related to the task of instruction for a specific subject and more descriptive of the characteristics of its acquisition. Thus, to devise adequate methods in the context of language study to satisfy the social demand for an individual to acquire a working knowledge of a language, one has to know exactly the definition of the term 'working knowledge of a language', and this presupposes a certain knowledge of psychology and linguistics.

The sources for constructing curriculum content at the level of the lesson remain the same as those at the level of constructing a school subject, and differ only in the way they are used. The latter distinction is determined by the function the study material performs in the teaching process, since that material serves as a means of instruction, in its immediate practical sense, for the teacher and a means of learning for the pupil.

At this level, one can see with particular clarity the distinction between science subjects and all the other subjects in using the materials of science.

Knowledge of teaching procedures determines a methodological configuration of study material which will serve as concrete norms for the activity of the teacher and pupils.

Psychological knowledge enables the structuring of the lesson according to the pattern of reasoning of pupils and their age, and plays a role in consolidating methodological principles. Certain psychological arguments and practices may even directly substantiate the application of educational activity, both in compiling and using the lesson. Thus, the psychological characterization of a problem situation may be directly employed in compiling the lesson, including certain types of learning problems.

Such are the chief characteristics of a didactic approach to the construction of the content of general education and to its theoretical definition. Listed below are the goals of a theory of curriculum content which is now being developed in accordance with the above approach: (a) to develop a theoretical concept of the content of general secondary education, taking into consideration social demands and socially-generated goals as well as the theoretical and concrete materials embodying the content; (b) to compile a scientific description of the object of curriculum content theory in terms of a multi-level system of categories such as 'composition', 'function' and 'structure'; (c) to study the methods to define and consolidate curriculum content level-by-level as an educational model of social goals.

In terms of practical results, the development of a theory of curriculum content involves: (a) the selection of methodological criteria for the development of a theory on the basis of a didactic approach; (b) furnishing didactic justification for subject content at school and for actually imparting school subjects in class, i.e. rationales for selecting and structuring study material in curricula and syllabuses.

* * *

In concluding this chapter, it appears logical to return to the principles underlying the compilation of the content of general secondary education, principles which follow the process of identification already outlined earlier. It is through the process of scientific research that the identification (and up-dating) of this approach to the construction of curriculum content becomes possible. It is through research, through solving actual problems in the development of curriculum content, that one is able to identify from the sum-total of normative concepts those which can be designated with certainty as principles, i.e. as standard definitions covering all the phenomena in the given field of research. The importance of these concepts for content construction will be demonstrated when we come to use them.

The first of the three basic principles underlying the development of content for general secondary education is a principle of *correspondence* — in all its elements and at all levels of its formulation — *to the demands of society*. All-round personality development being the chief goal of formal education under socialism, this principle means including into curriculum content those elements which support that development. It also means curriculum content going beyond the mere acquisition of knowledge and skills to covering such elements of social experience as creative activity and the ability to form one's own attitudes towards reality. It also assumes the inclusion of the above elements of curriculum content into every school subject, curriculum, syllabus and textbook. And finally, the same principle presupposes that the goal of all-round personality development should determine the place, function and, for that matter, content of every school subject in the context of general secondary education.

The principle of *unity of content and process in teaching* reflects the contribution of practice to the construction and theoretical substantiation of curriculum content. Earlier we referred to this unity in arguing that curriculum content only takes on its final form in the process of teaching. This principle is opposed to any one-sided approach to curriculum content which tends to isolate it from the educational context. This principle means, *inter alia*, designing the content of a school subject or any element of study material with regard to the existing methods, practices and possibilities, as well as including into curricula and textbooks not only content but also the methods whereby it should be imparted to and acquired by the pupils.

And finally, there is a principle of *structural unity of curriculum content* at all the levels of its construction, from the general forms down to its use in teaching.

This principle infers that curriculum content should not be defined (or finally expressed) as a mere accumulation of school subjects, curricula and syllabuses assembled in complete isolation, as was sometimes the case in the past. The compiler of a particular syllabus should have in mind a broad overview of the structure of the projected curriculum prior to actually putting pen to paper. This principle indicates the adoption of a common approach to the development of each particular school subject or any other piece of study material.

It also assumes identifying in broad outline connections between subjects already at the first level of content construction, i.e. prior to dealing with school subjects. In this case, when the structure of curriculum content is conceived as early as the level of theoretical conceptualization, the above connections may be designated as 'pre-subject'. At the subsequent levels of content construction they will, of course, acquire material substance. The advantage of this approach is a possibility to co-ordinate, at least in broad terms, school subjects with curricula content as a whole even *before* the subjects, appropriate syllabuses and textbooks have actually come into being.

This monograph is of necessity restricted to the basic, most urgent and specific problems encountered in developing a theory of curriculum content. The research that has been carried out naturally covered a wider spectrum of problems that were treated in greater detail. In fact, the present text is a summary of the final outcomes. The research was also concerned with: the present-day status of theory and practice concerning the content of general secondary education; the methodology of developing a theory underlying that content and associated problems; the goals and principles of general secondary education which could serve as criteria for the construction of education content; the sources and factors influencing content construction (social experience, types and branches of human activity, the process of revealing content, the way various types of content are acquired, the means and methods of teaching oriented towards imparting specific elements of content, etc.); the composition and structure of curriculum content at the different levels of its construction; with the polytechnical components of general secondary education; the units of content; the composition and construction of school subjects and their classification; didactic requirements for content and its reflection in curricula and textbooks. Most of these problems will come under theoretical scrutiny later in this book.

REFERENCES

1. Skatkin, M.N.; Kraevskij, V.V. *Soderžanie obščego srednego obrazovanija: problemy i perspektivy.* Moskva, Znanie, 1981. 96 p.
2. Makarenko, A.S. *Sočinenija. T.5.* Moskva, 1951, p. 441.
3. Babanskij, Ju.K. Ob aktualnyh problemah soveršenstvovanija obučenija v obščeobrazovatel'noj škole. *Sovetskaja pedagogika* (Moskva), no. 3, 1979, p. 3–10.
4. Judin, E.G. *Sistemnyj podhod i princip dejatel'nosti: metodologičeskie problemy sovremennoj nauki.* Moskva, 'Nauka', 1978.

5. *Op.cit.*, p. 41-46.
6. Mostepanenko, M.V. *Filosofija i metody naučnogo poznanija.* Leningrad, 1972, p. 153.
   Švyrev, V.S. Dialektika teoretičeskogo i empiričeskogo v sovremennoj nauke. *Kommunist* (Moskva), no. 14, 1977, p. 74.
7. Engel's, F. Principy kommunizma. *In:* Marks, K.; Engel's, F. *Sočinenija. T.4.* p. 336.
8. Gorskij, P.D.; Smirnov, S.N. Aktual'nye problemy dialektiko-materialističeskogo učenija o praktike i poznanii. *In: Praktika i poznanie.* Moskva, 'Nauka', 1973.
9. Lenin, V.I. Collected works. Vol. 38. 4th ed. Moscow, Foreign Language Publishing House, 1963, p. 213.
10. Vahtomin, N.K. *Genezis naučnogo znanija: fakt, ideja, teorija.* Moskva, 'Nauka', 1973.
11. Simonjan, E.A. *Edinstvo teorii i praktiki (filosofskij analiz).* Moskva, 'Nauka', 1980, p. 102.
12. Hirst, P.H. The nature and scope of educational theory. *In:* Langford, G.; O'Connor, J.D., eds. *New essays in the philosophy of education.* Boston, Mass., Routledge & Kegan Paul, 1973.
13. Kraevskij, V.V. *Problemy naučnogo obosnovanija obučenija (metodologi□ skij analiz).* Moskva, 'Pedagogika', 1977. 264 p.
14. Lenin, V.I. *Op.cit.*, p. 213.
15. Kline, M. Intellectuals and the schools: a case history. *Harvard educational review* (Cambridge, Mass.), vol. 36, no. 4, Fall 1966, p. 505-511.
16. Huebener, T. The new key is now off-key! *The modern language journal* (Menasha, Wis.), vol. 47, no. 4, December 1963, p. 357.
17. Dewey, J. *Psychology and social practice.* Chicago, University of Chicago Press, 1901. 42 p. (University of Chicago contributions to education, no. II).
18. *Ibid.*
19. James, W. *Talks to teachers on psychology.* New York, Holt, 1946.
20. Makarenko, A.S. *Sočinenija. T. VII.* Moskva, 1958, p. 402.
21. Handschin, C.H. *Methods of teaching modern languages.* Yonkers-on-Hudson, N.Y., 1923.
22. Marks, K. Tezisy o Fejerbahe. *In:* Marks, K.; Engel's, F. *Sočinenija. T.3.* p. 2.
23. Bueva, L.P. Problema dejatel'nosti ličnosti v Marksistskoj i buržuaznoj sociologii. *In: Istoričeskij materializm kak teorija social'nogo poznanija i dejatel'nosti.* Moskva, 1972, p. 43.
    Markarjan, E.S. Voprosy sistemnogo rassmotrenija kul'tury i čelovečeskoj dejatel'nosti. *In: Istoričeskij materializm kak teorija social'nogo poznanija i dejatel'nosti.* Moskva, 1972.
24. United Kingdom. Department of Education and Science. H.M. Inspectorate. *Curriculum 11-16. Working papers by HM Inspectorate: a contribution to current debate.* London, Department of Education and Science, 1977. 84 p.
25. United Kingdom. Department of Education and Science. *Local authority arrangements for the school curriculum: report on the Circular 14/77 review,* by the Department of Education and Science and Welsh Office. London, H.M.S.O., 1979. 197 p.
26. United Kingdom. Department of Education and Science. *The school curriculum.* London, 1981.
27. Hirst, P. The logic of curriculum development. *In:* Galton, M., ed. *Curriculum change: the lessons of a decade.* Leicester, United Kingdom, Leicester University Press, 1980, p. 9-10.
28. *Ibid.*
29. Beardsley, M.C. Aesthetic theory and educational theory. *In:* Smith, R.A., ed. *Aesthetic concepts and education.* Chicago, Ill., University of Illinois Press, 1970. p. 5.

46   The theory of curriculum content in the USSR

30. Abul'hanova, K.A. *O sub'ekte psihičeskoj dejatel'nosti: metodologičeskie problemy psihologii.* Moskva, 'Nauka', 1973, p. 268.
31. Lingart, J. *Process i struktura čelovečeskogo učenija.* Moskva, 'Progress', 1970, p. 69.
32. Talyzina, N.F. Kibernetika i pedagogika. *In: Problemy socialističeskoj pedagogiki.* Red. kollegija. A.I. Markuševič et al. Moskva, 'Pedagogika', 1973, p. 146.
33. O'Connor, J.D. The nature and scope of educational theory. *In:* Langford, G.; O'Connor, J.D., eds. *New essays in the philosophy of education.* Boston, Mass., Routledge & Kegan Paul, 1973, p. .
34. Trubnikov, N.N. *O kategorijah 'cel'', 'sredstvo', 'rezul'tat'.* Moskva, 'Vysšaja škola', 1968, p. 92.
35. Venable, T.C. *Philosophical foundations of the curriculum.* Chicago, Ill., Rand McNally, 1967, p. 21.
36. Hirst, P. The logic of curriculum development. *In:* Galton, M., ed. *Curriculum change: the lessons of a decade.* Leicester, United Kingdom, Leicester University Press, 1980, p. 16.
37. Bueva, L.P. *Op.cit.*
38. Matjuškin, A.M. *Problemnye situacii v myslenii i obučenii.* Moskva, 'Pedagogika', 1972. 208 p.
39. Gott, V.S.; Ursul, A.D. *Obščenaučnye ponjatija i ih rol' v poznanii.* Moskva, 'Znanie', 1975, p. 30-32.
40. Vahtomin, N.K. *Op.cit.*, p. 253.
41. Klimentenko, A.D.; Miroljubova, A.A., eds. *Teoretičeskie osnovy metodiki obučenija inostrannym jazykam v srednej skole.* Moskva, 'Pedagogika', 1981, p. 16, 17-32.
42. Miroljubova, A.A.; Rahmanova, I.V.; Četlin, V.S., eds. *Obščaja metodika obučenija inostrannym jazykam v srednej škole.* Moskva, 'Prosveščenie', 19 , p. 72-73.
43. Wilkins, D.A. Notional syllabuses revisited. *Applied linguistics* (Oxford, United Kingdom), vol. 2, no. 1, 1981, p. 83.
44. Ek, J.A. van. *Functional and notional syllabus.* Strasbourg, 1976.

CHAPTER II
Composition and structure of content for general education

1. INTERPRETING THE DEFINITION OF CONTENT

Writer Leonid Leonov tells the story of two craftsmen who were contracted to pave the public square of a city with stone mosaic. One of them got ready with his materials, squatted down and set to work. The other climbed up the city tower, took a good look at the square, sized up its dimensions, configuration and proportions, made a mental layout and only then began laying stones.

Whatever research one may be doing, it appears rational to situate the object in a wider perspective, since the broader the system the higher is the vantage point and the more vivid are the individual elements and their relationships. Strictly speaking, curriculum content has hitherto eluded consistent theoretical scrutiny even though educationists have come up with quite a few useful concepts concerning it.

As was stated in Chapter I, curriculum content is susceptible of formulation at several levels, the first of them being that of theory. It is at this level that one determines the source of content, its basic structure, the functions of each element and the links between them. Such an approach is absolutely essential to the construction of curriculum content in order to satisfy current social demands and goals, of which all-round development of the personality is the principal one. A theoretical definition of curricula includes a certain number of guidelines for future content as well as taking into account the existing situation. One cannot reconcile oneself to the idea that any substantive portion of general education should fail to reflect the guidelines on content and its relationships with other subjects. Neither can one accept the idea of a school subject which is in discord with the composition of curriculum content at the planning level. The composition of study materials, including textbooks, work books, and manuals on educational technology and methodology, should also be brought into alignment with the composition of curriculum content as a whole.

Since the origins of teaching, curriculum content has been conceived from the point of view of its composition by subjects (reading, writing, arithmetic, physics, history, etc.) on the one hand, and from the perspective of those elements which are common to all subjects on the other. According to the second viewpoint, curriculum content is a system of knowledge and skills. The two viewpoints have not always coexisted in harmony and the study of their partnership may elucidate how to solve the problem of subject composition in a manner in line with modern scientific achievements.

The study of curriculum content has hitherto progressed along the direction diametrically opposed to that which appears best for modern didactics to follow in its bid to define the compilation of content and thus meet the demands placed upon education by modern society. Prior to the advent of the school as a social institution in its own right, content originally took the form — whether deliberately or not — of instruction with a view to satisfying such basic human pursuits as hunting, tool-making and, later, cultivation and craftsmanship. Habits to be learned reflected the social demands for attaining definite, above all practical, skills. Content was intentionally reduced to the comprehension of a few skills which were most needed to perform certain domestic and productive activities essential to maintaining life in the literal, material sense.

With the school becoming a social institution, greater attention was given — in imparting curriculum content to the younger generation — to the particular functions that different social strata were expected to perform in society. Young people from different groups were now taught with an eye to such particular activities as farming, craftsmanship, knighthood, priesthood, administrative and military service, or several of these areas combined, even though the curriculum was still regarded as a unit combining several subjects. In the centuries that followed, there was an increase in the division of labour and social functions which resulted in a corresponding increase in the number of different branches.

Associated with the usual school subjects there have always been certain branches of social or practical activities. At all times, these activities — understood as drawn from real life — were a primary source of curriculum content, i.e. of content and not of education as such, since to teach a practical activity it has first to be educationally adapted to the process of learning. Throughout history practical activities have always been included in curricula, since teaching from its very beginning has had as its principal mission the conservation and development of society by building on what already exists. This conservation and development is always relevant, based on everyday objects and experiences and, once it has been divided into branches corresponding to these objects and experiences, forms part of the objectives of education. All the other results of teaching are subordinate to this goal and have been derived from the development of culture in all its aspects.

It is for these reasons that practical activities to this day remain a source for the compilation of curricula. Indeed, each subject embodies one or more practical activities, while the total of subjects in all types of educational institutions span the entire range of social experience accumulated by mankind throughout history — experience which is divided into specialities to be passed on from generation to generation.

Thus, in our model of curriculum content, it seems important that all social experience should be reflected somewhere in school subjects or in some other form of educational activity (such as out-of-school clubs or other groups). And since general secondary education seeks to initiate the pupil into those activities which will be vital for him to perform successfully as a citizen and a qualified person, one has to assemble from all branches of activity only those skills needed for general education — not losing sight of all-round personality development as the ultimate goal.

However, the approach which consists of dividing curriculum content into branches, useful as it may appear for socializing the young, has for some time been felt to be inadequate. This shortcoming first came to light when the teaching of skills was no longer considered adequate in preparing the pupil to function as a member of society. At one time there was a movement which considered it possible to mould in man a view of reality without resorting to active methods. This movement included *inter alia* religious and anthropological myths. Such content had a dubious role to play as regards the replication of society. A concomitant increase in the complexity of activities meant that only a professional presentation, a skilful explanation, could in short explain the subjects; the subject could only be made explicit and plain by presenting it in class. Thus, there were grounds for detaching knowledge from action, for separate treatment. Already Plato sought to define knowledge as a 'true opinion or an image'[1].

The discovery that knowledge can be relatively independent of activity, that knowledge may not be related to activity at all, and that the acquisition of any skill had to be preceded by the acquisition of theoretical knowledge all led to content being differentiated, i.e. that part of content which is common to all specialities had to be singled out. Curriculum content was now broken down into knowledge, useful habits and skills, and defined as a system of knowledge and skills. Pestalozzi clearly perceived this differentiation, but — even though still remaining in use — it is no longer looked upon as adequate today.

In historical terms, the definition and explanation of curriculum content has developed 'on a vertical plane', i.e. on the basis of branches of activity embodied in school subjects and revealed over time, as well as 'on a horizontal plane', i.e. on the basis of the composition of each subject. It is the latter approach that falls within the province of didactics.

Didactics is expected to demonstrate common ground in the composition of individual subjects as far as the practice and methodology of instruction are concerned. To perform this function it should first provide a firm answer to the question of what the content of education should be like for all subjects together and for each subject apart.

In the modern educational sciences, curriculum content is more often than not defined as a system of knowledge and skills providing a basis for the development of pupils' learning potential and for their socialization. This definition remains vague as to the exact conditions under which knowledge and skills are supposed to enable the pupils to develop their potential and become socialized. Such results are certainly not attainable solely through acquiring knowledge and skills. One can have all the knowledge in the world and still be totally uncreative. In the words of Democritus, the accumulation of knowledge is no contribution to wisdom. We all know that a mere grasp of the accepted ,moral code is no guarantee of acceptable behaviour. Since the acquisition of knowledge and skills does not automatically lead to the blossoming of one's intellectual potential, creative self-fulfilment and socialization, we still need to identify that missing ingredient of curriculum content which should make this goal attainable. How then to determine the composition of curriculum content and on what particular objective should we concentrate in analysing this composition?

2. SOCIAL EXPERIENCE AS A SOURCE

Prior to answering the above question, one has to determine what a core curriculum comprises in terms of theoretical didactics. In order to arrive at the correct answer it seems appropriate to follow the reverse direction to that in which curriculum content has developed throughout history. In other words, initially it is proposed to study the theory of curriculum content and then to use the resultant concept as a reference by which to judge the present situation, whatever form it may have assumed (an individual subject, a group of related subjects, etc.) as a criterion of what core content comprises. Thus, a theoretical concept of curriculum content will emerge that will act as a tool with which to construct core curricula at all levels.

At this point, it appears relevant to recapitulate certain assumptions. The general function of instruction has invariably been to pass on to the younger generation social experience (or culture) for the purpose of replication and further development. If young people were not adequately trained, culture could be neither replicated nor developed and hence any further existence of society would be compromised. Every society at every stage of human history has sought to pass on to the younger generation (and, objectively speaking, succeeded in so doing) its socio-cultural heritage. However, owing to social stratification the various elements of culture were passed on discriminately, i.e. a particular social stratum of young people inherited a particular element of their cultural heritage. Thus, one was destined to fulfil a different function depending on one's social class. Social stratification resulted in curricula content being different for different social groups. Therefore, it was superfluous to select all the elements for curriculum content; the appropriate selection could be made for each social group depending on the demands placed by society on that group. Socialist society was the first in history to concern itself with passing on to the younger generation all the elements of experience accumulated by the broader society. Of its very nature, socialist society could no longer deny any elements of experience to any particular social stratum. Indeed, it was the first to ever tackle the problem.

Since the social goal of teaching under socialism consists of imparting the entire cultural heritage to all the younger generation, culture is now equated with curriculum content and it is the analysis of culture that should reveal the structural elements of content.

The goal of teaching is to make the cultural (or social) heritage available to each member of society. All acquired personality traits are nothing but acquired personality content. A trained pupil has acquired a certain amount of content. The degree of training depends on the amount of content the pupil has acquired; the nature of being trained depends on the nature of acquired content; and since in order to reproduce culture satisfactorily the content of formal education has to measure up to the content of culture, culture becomes a point of departure in defining that content.

This argument seems to bear out Davydov's contention that 'all that comprises the end-product of an individual's activity, as well as all the conditions in which this activity takes place, originally existed as a social model outside and independently of that individual'[2].

Throughout history, man has built up an immense cultural wealth — material and spiritual — and developed to an astonishing degree his intellectual capacity. This intellectual wealth has taken generations to accrue[3]. Every new generation has had to acquire not only the methods to draw on that heritage but also the methods to change inherited conditions — methods which are themselves inherited and at the same time serve as the means to devise still newer methods to carry out activity and change conditions. We now have to go beyond the mere grasp of a few patterns of practical and mental activity into the habit of discarding them, changing them and creating new patterns. All this complexity of activity patterns comprises the human cultural heritage. There is nothing outside the domain of culture that can become part of curriculum content, and vice-versa. In an education system based on humanistic principles, curriculum content must embrace all the elements of culture.

At this point we are confronted with two problems: that of defining culture for the purposes of the present discourse, and that of selecting an adequate criterion for analysing culture into elements.

Of the definitions of culture most frequently met with in literature one is likely to come across the following: 'Culture is the sum-total of material and spiritual values amassed by mankind in the process of socio-historical evolution'[4].

In view of the difficulty of defining culture and the sheer number of attempts at defining it already made — 257 according to some sources[5], 164 according to others[6], counting only the attempts made up to the early 1930s — we will limit our discourse to a single point in the above-mentioned definition. Culture is studied by numerous sciences, such as philosophy, sociology and cultural anthropology. Each of these has a particular field of interest within this sphere. This is applicable to the educational sciences. A particular object of study for the realm of culture is the composition of culture or those elements of content which are fit to be imparted to the individual. The educational sciences are concerned with personality development and hence with the influences upon it. Therefore culture is approached with a view to selecting items that can be imparted to and acquired by the individual. To identify that content, culture is viewed in terms of activity, since it is activity alone that one imparts to the individual. In emphasizing individual elements we imply human, intellectual, emotional and behavioural qualities, to the exclusion of the physical. The individual in this definition cannot be taught material culture. He can only be imparted with activity through the medium of material culture, for which purpose the individual is expected to learn the structure and means of producing material objects such as, for instance, machine-tools, buildings and instruments. To acquire spiritual (disembodied) culture the individual has likewise to perform a learning activity. Culture manifests itself as the sum-total of activities, and can be acquired through man's learning activity. An individual's culture can be measured by his mastery of the content of cultural activity. Culture, as it is embodied in activity, is shared by the entire living generation and is that social experience of society which can only be imparted to the younger generation by instructing it in the family and in the school. Social experience is nothing but a the total of material and ideational means and methods of activity which man develops in the process of maintaining society and which can be shared by every individual. The social experience of the present generation embodying cultural content amassed through the centuries is the only source of the content of formal or any other type of education. Outside social experience there is nothing that can possibly become part of curriculum content. In curriculum content there is nothing that can be gained anywhere outside social experience.

Indeed, the acquisition of a specific culture by an individual is only possible if that individual learns specific cultural traits. By the acquisition of specific traits an individual absorbs culture through activity, as an active process, this being only possible through the individual's own activity. Hence, the acquisition of culture is only possible through activity carried out for the purpose of learning the methods, results and products of activity. Culture amassed in this way becomes the social experience of living generations.

Yet, the scope and elements of social experience to be acquired by an individual are determined historically and depend on the quantity of amassed culture and also on social conditions. In prehistoric society, with its extremely limited social structure and in the absence of social stratification, every individual had little or no difficulty acquiring the entire social experience. Any instructed person in prehistoric society was, by definition, master of the entire social experience. As culture progressed, the ratio between the quantity of culture acquired by an individual and the entire social experience (equated with the entire culture) changed. Thus, an individual became master of social experience in only one area, however broad. For quite some time, for instance, a peasant could be master of all that was known about agriculture. At the dawn of craftsmanship, when it was still part of agriculture, each craftsman was master of all or nearly all the trades. The higher the development of craftsmanship the greater was its specialization and the wider the gap between personal acquisition of culture and society's total social experience. The acquisition of the entire social experience by any one person was no longer possible because of its sheer size. No less an obstacle was the social differentiation resulting in discrete social groups having access only to specific areas of culture. Thus, peasants and artisans were barred from the social experience of knighthood, and vice versa. As a rule, serfs were barred from participating in administration or religious activity, etc.

Since an individual can never hope to acquire the whole of social experience, and since the conservation and development of culture do not depend on any single individual either, one should select from the vast body of social experience those essential elements which are common to all branches of culture, that are omnipresent, to its tiniest unit (such as an individual sporadic act). This selection is guided by the above-mentioned definition of culture and the social experience embodying it. All-round personality development can only be achieved by acquiring those essentials which comprise the core of culture.

In situations where education is available to all, regardless of sex, race, national origin or social status, it is necessary for the education of every individual to contribute to the conservation and further development of culture. To achieve this one should identify in the cultural heritage those typical elements which are to become part of education, whatever its form and irrespective of the intended profession. Thus, one has to choose social experience as an object for study if one is to define the constituent elements of curriculum content. Otherwise, teaching will tend to become inadequate, as one can see by looking back over the centuries of formal education and socialization.

Yet, prior to doing this, it is absolutely essential to choose a vantage point from which to study social experience with a view to identifying its recurring and constant elements. There is an obvious need for an adequate criterion for selection. As long as our interest is focused upon social experience to be passed on from generation to generation this criterion means nothing more than to identify those factors in the content of each element which determine its function in the process of replication and further development of culture. The unique content and function of each element in maintaining culture, the fact that one element cannot be replaced by another to perform the same function, are not merely a criterion of the existence of each element, but indeed the justification.

Through identifying the constituent elements of social experience one identifies the unique elements of curriculum content, since the latter is analogous in composition to the former and is the sole source of selecting curriculum content.

Thus, the selection of elements of social experience amounts to the selection of elements of curriculum content.

3. KNOWLEDGE AND MODES OF ACTIVITY

In order to assess the content of culture as the sum-total of activity it appears logical to select as a basic unit an intentional act performed by an individual. Let us suppose that each individual act is composed of elements that are identical with the entire social experience, which we define as all activities. Each intentional act is a complete unit, since it is meant to attain a definite purpose. Each individual act has a structure and also forms part of the structure of social experience (the sum-total of activities).

It is possible to identify four constituent elements of culture as well as of each individual act (the tiniest structural unit of social experience). Each operation of intentional activity presupposes foreknowledge of the aim, method, means and likely outcome. Accordingly, *the first element of social experience is knowledge* already gained by society of the natural environment, of society, technology, man and such activities as enable the application of knowledge and the transformation of reality.

That this element is the first and indispensable one is borne out by the fact that the understanding and transformation of reality is confined to the process of purposeful and intentional action. A purposeful action by definition must be preceded by a certain amount of knowledge as to the possible outcomes of this action and the methods involved. Such knowledge is absolutely essential in the replication of culture. It stands to reason that every action must be motivated. Yet, the motivation of a definite, purposive action stems from the knowledge about it and its effects. Thus, knowledge of the reality (the object) and of the method of object-related activity is an essential prerequisite to action itself. Some of the characteristics of that knowledge seem relevant to the present discussion. Generally speaking, knowledge is by its nature non-uniform. There are different kinds of knowledge. The kinds of knowledge of interest to us here are terms and designations, facts, laws, theories, methodological knowledge and evaluative knowledge. Terms and designations serve to categorize an object or an aggregate of knowledge. For instance, this purpose is served by language which embodies knowledge and provides formal structure to concepts. Factual knowledge is a basis for any other knowledge in that it is a direct reflection of reality.

Even though laws may reflect only part of all facts, in the mind of a student of these facts such laws serve to demonstrate that they do not exist in isolation from each other.

Theories cover a large number of facts and the laws that bind them together; they systematize individual mental images and qualify phenomena by explaining and defining them.

Methodological knowledge includes information on the methods, process and background of learning, on the methods of science, and on the methods and techniques of activity.

And finally, evaluative knowledge establishes norms for assuming an attitude to objects, an attitude which ascribes a value to the relative importance of these objects (including various types of knowledge) in a grouping or a system. Evaluative knowledge is conducive to forming an individual's attitude to reality, to laying down a system of personal values and to establishing the degree of importance of a definite activity for that individual.

In the present state of the development of knowledge, all the above types of knowledge are likely to influence one another and, in their sum total, are capable of influencing the individual that has acquired them. Only as an integrated whole can all types of knowledge perform their functions in the lives of people. If one type of knowledge is ignored, all the rest cannot perform their functions. Indicated below are three of these types of knowledge capable of moulding personality.

The first function of knowledge in the above sense is to serve as a basis for the cognition of reality, i.e. an *ontological* function. Once he is born into the world, an individual develops ideas about the objects surrounding him, then about their interconnections, about human relations and, ultimately, about his own place in the world vis-à-vis other people. Without developing these ideas, human life would be unthinkable. The ideas one forms about the world may be either restricted or broad enough to determine one's area of activity. It is incumbent upon the school to create in the pupil's mind a general image of the world simple enough for him to acquire and at the same time in keeping with modern scientific attitudes, an image that, if thoroughly comprehended, should broaden the pupil's understanding and orientation.

The second function of knowledge — guidance — means that knowledge serves as a guide in choosing the line of activity, whether practical or aesthetic. Being aware of the laws and trends of the development of phenomena and their explanation, an individual is in a position to select the optimum methods and principles of action. Certain kinds of knowledge may serve as norms for practical and learning activity, taking the form of rules, recommendations and standardized procedures.

And finally, *the third function of knowledge* may serve a basis to acquire an attitude to reality, since in the absence of knowledge of an object and its relative importance one cannot put a value on it. This is the *evaluative* function of knowledge.

Neither knowledge to guide activity nor knowledge of the methods of activity is equivalent to the skill to use that knowledge in real-life situations. Knowledge means only the theoretical mastery of an object[7]. To acquire an active mastery, and thus turn knowledge of an object into a skill or a useful habit, it is necessary to employ a method of activity and thus acquire practical experience. Possessing this experience is not the same as having knowledge of these methods. Thus, in the absence of practical experience, knowledge of the methods of writing letters will not be enough to write them. Knowledge of the methods of comparison is not enough to develop a skill of comparison, for that one needs practical experience. Imagine giving a dynamometer to a child and explaining how to measure his grip. For all the explanation, the child would handle the instrument in such a manner that the readings on the counter would repeatedly fall far below his actual force. It would only be after several attempts that the child would succeed in correctly manipulating the instrument so that the readings are more accurate.

The child's experience, the rate and degree at which he gains that experience, always remain (within certain limits) subjective. Yet, the content of experience in acquiring modes of behaviour in practice remains (within certain limits) objective, outside the child's mind until he makes it his own. When it has been gained through individual practice, what has been learned differs from knowledge of an activity obtained from an outside source. This content is that accretion to human experience, which — as well as knowledge — individuals gain as a result of repeatedly practising methods of acquisition and application, i.e. by practising activity. The content of this experience may escape conscious perception altogether, i.e. it may not be consciously established, unlike knowledge itself which is invariably fixed in one's mind. A small child performs the operation of a mental calculation without any outside help and without any knowledge of the pattern of the operation, i.e. entirely on the basis of practical experience of actually conducting that operation, communicating with adults and reproducing the operation in the same way as adults.

Experience in using active methods, it is worth repeating, is a kind of special content which can never be fully mastered simply by having acquired knowledge of these methods. 'Knowing' is not yet 'being able to do'. Typically, considerable practical effort is put in by those participating in education before they succeed in learning to perform certain actions such as reading, writing, comparing, etc. Thus, *the second element of culture is skill*; that part of social experience which is gained through using the methods of intellectual and practical activities already known to society, i.e. experience in reproducing those methods which are already known to society and mastered by individuals. These activities serve to reproduce the answers to cognitive and practical problems which have already been solved. Whenever one reproduces the methods to calculate the circumference of a circle, measure the temperature, build the next house, carry out the sowing and harvesting, etc., one actually reproduces experience.

Availing oneself of the first element (knowledge) does not automatically make available the second element (skill) and, vice-versa; the second element can neither replace nor cause to form the first element. Knowledge without skill is not enough to reproduce culture, since it is skill (classified as the second element) that enables culture-reproducing activity. Such is the social function performed by the second element.

Psychological research indicates that having knowledge of an activity cannot be equated with having practical experience in using that knowledge. The nature of interaction of skills, which is independent of having knowledge of activities, may serve as the proof that these two elements of social experience are independent of each other. Sometimes skills, i.e. experience in carrying out certain activities, may hamper the acquisition of another experience. For example, there is a phenomenon known as interference of skills or negative transfer, of which numerous examples are cited in the literature of psychology. Thus, drawing lines from the top downwards hampers the learner's progress in drawing lines from the bottom up during lessons on draftsmanship; motorists find it hard to change from left-hand to right-hand drive traffic, etc. There are cases to the contrary as well, when knowledge of old and new activities differs but the similarity of activities covered by that knowledge may help an adept of the old activity to master the new one. Thus, experience of working with a file helps master the manipulation of a hacksaw.

Additional experiments favour the conclusion that experience in implementing an activity is independent of knowledge concerning that activity. In one such experiment, by pressing the appropriate buttons on a control panel and watching a display, the pupil had to flash lights of the same colour as the lights flashed by the experimenter. At first, the intervals between flashes were rather long, but gradually, as the pupil mastered the trick, the response time became less. The predetermined time of response was achieved only after almost 180 repetitions[8]. This pattern signifies that a mere knowledge of an activity and even its persistent repetition fails to give one experience enough to perform it faultlessly in practice. Such qualities as skilfulness, reflex action, fast response and adaptation to changing conditions are not acquired through knowledge but depend on a quite different set of experiences.

Whether the mastery of an activity is hampered by the interference of skills upon each other or promoted by their positive interaction, acquired knowledge of an activity has nothing in common with either.

A skill is knowledge of a mode of activity combined with experience in using that mode. Experience is a mere adjunct to knowledge. The consistent repetition of an activity does not increase the quantity of information gained but does improve the level of performance, and that performance may well be subconscious, not fixed in the mind as any piece of knowledge. Whether learning to drive a nail home with a single hammer blow or learning to arrive at a mental conclusion, a child performs the preparatory activity according to an acquired habit without being conscious himself of how he performs it. Or else, a child may gain experience consciously and for a purpose, but the act of gaining experience cannot result in a mastery of an activity without being associated with the appropriate practical experience. Thus, the second element of social experience is the experience in using means of activity, this experience reproducing culture in a manner completely different from that of knowledge.

4. EXPERIENCE IN CREATIVE ACTIVITY

Besides the ability to reproduce the solution to problems which have already been solved, one may be faced with finding the solution to new problems. These latter problems may differ in complexity and their solution may depend on varying degrees of novelty. A method that has already been used to solve a problem in one field may be applied in the same field but under different conditions. Alternatively, there may be a need to apply methods in an entirely different field and, prior to so doing, it may be necessary in each case to choose a particular method from a particular domain to be applied to the solution of a particular problem. In still other cases, the problem in hand may be so novel in character that its solution rules out all known methods as unsuitable or impracticable, and calls for an entirely new approach. Since man, throughout history, has been haunted by problems which, unless solved, would have impaired progress, human society has gained experience in transferring problem-solving methods to new settings and adapting them accordingly, borrowing methods from one field to be applied in an entirely different one, combining and recombining various methods together, designing altogether new methods, visualizing known problems from an entirely different angle and, last but not least, posing new problems.

Experience in creative skill has accumulated gradually with the development of culture. Creative thinking has been enriched with the expansion of material objects made by man. Knowledge and skills are not only becoming more refined but also, from time to time, being replaced. In short, experience in creativity gets richer as culture as a whole develops.

Human society has gradually gained experience in creativity through practical contact with reality, which is borne out by the entire history of science. Copernicus, Bacon and Galileo demonstrated that it is necessary to verify experimentally what has been perceived by the senses and reasoned out by speculation. This led to a major step forward in the development of cognitive abilities, resulting in progress in the ability to design methods to check on theoretical hypotheses. Ohm's experiments with the substitution of a source of current prompted a method for a random verification of ideas, which was another step forward in our experience of what is now known as alternative reasoning[9].

The gradual accumulation of social experience in creative thinking is further exemplified in the way a child develops. As a child grows, so do the forms, procedures and mechanisms of his thinking. This is an illustration in miniature of the way the entire social process of acquiring the forms, procedures and mechanisms of reasoning has developed from one epoch to the next.

The third element of social experience and curriculum content — experience in creativity (which is essential in a search for solutions to new problems and in transforming reality) has a content different from that of the first two elements. If it were not so, any individual who had gained any knowledge and skills would become creative. If individual creative potential depended on the quantity of knowledge acquired by any one individual, any modern schoolchild — as one educationist put it — would be more creative than Aristotle, since the former *knows* more than the latter. And vice-versa; there are quite a few people with knowledge far inferior to that of experts in the same field, but this does not prevent them from working in a far more creative manner. The history of labour, whether agricultural or industrial, is a history of creative effort on the part of illiterate, toiling masses through millenia. Indeed, it is not the quantity of knowledge that really matters.

Maybe everything depends on innate abilities. People are born with different talents — qualitatively and quantitatively. Do we need to worry about everyone's self-fulfilment? Would it not be sufficient to grant every member of society the freedom to study, listen to the radio, watch films and read any publications, ...and just to stop at that? Would it not automatically mean creative self-fulfilment for everybody if they succeeded in acquiring all the knowledge imparted in school, all the socially useful skills and habits?

Regretfully, this is not the case. Despite the fact that acquiring knowledge does develop reasoning, neither knowledge received second-hand nor skills mastered according to an established pattern are essential to self-fulfilment. If one gets into the habit of acquiring knowledge and skills second-hand, one's innate creative abilities may, in fact, get blunted.

A man untrained to think for himself but trained to accept all that is fed to him in a pre-digested form sooner or later loses his natural aptitude. Therefore society is legitimately concerned with introducing the younger generation to creativity. Psychological findings demonstrate that, at a particular stage in development, a child is responsive to a particular type of activity, whether emotional, motor or intellectual. So if a child is not trained to use intellectual activity at the right time, he is likely to miss an opportunity which it will be difficult to compensate for in subsequent years.

In short, one should be taught creativity from the cradle, a subject just as teachable as knowledge and skills, even though in a different way.

What then is experience in creativity; what is its content; what are the particulars of creative activity?

One is likely to come to the point at once by turning to the controversy which once arose between the school of thought prevailing in Soviet psychology and Jean Piaget. The latter maintained that mental development, whatever its stage or level, was immanent to a child's age and had no connection whatsoever with the nature of teaching. 'Whenever adults are trying to impose on a child mathematical concepts not consonant with its age, the child will acquire them only on attaining the appropriate mental age which he cannot attain ahead of time'[10].

The Soviet psychologists hold a different view (from which we proceed in the present discourse and which has been logically derived from a didactic analysis of the problem).

Gal'perin and El'konin write:

That which Piaget takes to be instruction in the narrow sense is a product of communicating second-hand knowledge and a second-hand method; the questions a child asks (logic of constructing an object and object-related activity) remain unanswered, the child is acquiring only 'knowledge and skills', while new and more sophisticated structures of thinking are formed only when the child comes to understand for himself the inner logic of objects and object-related activities[11].

Even before these authors, Rubinštejn had demonstrated that 'development' was one thing and the content of knowledge and skills another, the former implying not a co-ordination of procedures, but a 'culture of internal processes'[12]. But what is the content of the 'culture of internal processes'? Where does one go from there? And what does this 'culture' derive from? Does it derive from acquiring a content occurring outside the acquirer (as is the case with knowledge and activity), or does it derive from imparting to the acquirer specially organized knowledge which will mould him in accordance with contents? Yet, as we already know, in reality acquiring content does not inevitably result in a shift named 'development' and even if this content is acquired, that shift or 'development' is not necessarily attainable to the same degree. The degree of attainment in this case will depend on the organization of the content of the knowledge and activity method which is imparted. Not all content can result in a shift, a change in development; only specially organized content can do so. But if that is the case, it is fair to conclude that teaching the content of knowledge will have varying outcomes depending on variety in the organization of teaching.

Since there is nothing in personality content which does not exist in social experience, social experience being perceived and modified in the mind of an individual possessing that personality, it is fair to conclude that, in the case of a change in personality development, the content was acquired from social experience. This latter content differs from that of knowledge and skills. It can only be acquired because development is always expressed materially and because this material content of development is so organized as to embody a new content, that of creativity. This content, the acquisition of which is the most stimulating to development, has accumulated in social experience through practical activity in society, through the creative solution by mankind of intellectual and practical problems. Being part of individual experience, it is embodied in the very structure of problems posed by creative individuals, in the very configuration of such structures, this configuration being transmitted from generation to generation.

Hence, there is a need to define the content of experience in creative activity gained by mankind up to the present moment,and those structures of creative activity which embody that experience, in order to be able to govern consciously its transmission from generation to generation.

Two basic trends can be identified in the vast number of books on the psychology of creativity, some stressing the most typical aspects in the biographies of outstanding scholars and artists, other emphasizing the creative process as such. Thus, many authors concentrate on the personalities of creative individuals stressing personality patterns, such as a taste for challenging problems, a passion for simplifying complex problems, an openness to the opinions of others, an inclination to self-analysis, perseverance, etc. Some of the authors even go so far as to insist that being an orphan is a statistically significant factor in becoming a scientist. In view of our specific preoccupation, we have to limit ourselves to creativity as a process, and its content.

The aim of the present discussion is to select from the literature what is most typical in creative activity with special regard to the process by which it unfolds and, above all, that which comprises social experience and that minimum which is to be imparted to the pupil.

What are the typical traits of creativity stressed in the literature? There is a consensus of opinion that creative activity means not merely general aptitudes but a combination of specific aptitudes. Thus, Taylor et al.[13] stress personal energy, resourcefulness and ingenuity, intellectual honesty and straightforwardness, interest in knowing facts and principles, flexibility in interpreting facts, independence of judgement, intuition, etc. Attention is focused on those qualities which lend a special colouring to individual creative activity, those conditions under which this activity proceeds, without, however, much stress on the content- and process-related side of the activity in question.

In a report from a symposium held in Michigan[14] stress is laid not only on such traits of a creatively-minded individual as originality, unusual thinking, an aptitude for quick learning, flexibility in dealing with others, industriousness, an inclination to go it alone, a capacity to enjoy unpredictable situations, etc., but also on such traits of creativity proper as discarding all non-essentials, composing complex structures out of simple elements (synthesis), dividing phenomena or situations into elements (analysis), recombining elements, discarding time-tested methods or theories, openness to new facts, etc.

Some of the above traits were emphasized in earlier publications. Thus, Spearman lays special stress on the ability to single out what really matters to the exclusion of non-essentials[15]. Another author who dwells on discarding non-essential information in creative activity is Berlyne[16]. A group of authors[17] believe that creativity means to apply an existing structure in a new situation or in broadening a field of application. Others believe that an important manifestation of creative activity is the ability to grasp the essential in a field or situation under study. They tend to connect that ability with such traits as resourcefulness, ingenuity, originality, a quick grasp of the problem in hand, an ability to give up an accepted, habitual view, discarding non-essentials, an aptitude for synthesis, recombination, etc.[18].

An ability to pose new problems or see new problems in a traditional setting is considered essential in a creative mind.

The United States' authors writing on the subject generally admit that not a single issue pertaining to the creative process, the criteria of creativity and the ways in which creative abilities unfold has so far been solved (see for instance, an opinion expressed by MacLeod in a summary annexed to a collection entitled 'Contemporary approaches to creative thinking'[19]).

This problem is also dealt with in Soviet publications on psychology and the history of science. Thus, Samarin believes that a major manifestation of creativity is the ability to notice common features in different phenomena, as well as essential differences in largely identical objects[20]. Gurova tends to see signs of creativity in the ability to take one's bearings in a problem situation, persevere towards a desirable end in the absence of any established pattern to follow, and also in the ability to advance and verify hypotheses[21]. Lejtes stresses the importance of industriousness, interpreting it as an aptitude for work[22]. Some Soviet authors stress the ability to find alternatives in problem-oriented situations as a manifestation of creative thinking.

Menčinskaja classifies as creative the abilities to change patterns of behaviour, to orient research in a desired direction, to discard trite solutions and to modify approaches in problem solving[23].

Proceeding from published and experimental data from formal education (only covered to a limited extent in the references), we devoted our attention to those characteristics of creative activity (with special stress on its process side) the acquisition of which appears to be essential to the proper education of pupils[13 to 40]. In this discourse, the chief stress is neither on the characteristics of a creative personality, nor on the conditions under which creativity takes place, but on the qualitative features of creative activity proper with particular reference to dynamics as revealed in the process of creativity. The very configuration of learning structures depends on identifying what is really important from among a multitude of heterogeneous and homogeneous characteristics.

We sought, *inter alia*, to present these selected characteristics in such a way as to stress the need to provide a basis for moulding an independent and creative attitude to the object under scrutiny. A conscious formation of the above features should provide the pupils with a bare minimum of creative procedures and with the prospect of gaining more in the future (to a varying degree for different children, of course). This is all the more important since ignoring the need for the deliberate inculcation of creative procedures might hamper their acquisition on a large scale. We know that much from experience.

Summarized below are process-related features comprising the content of experience in creativity:

1. An ability to transfer knowledge and skills from one situation to another independently and irrespective of the gulf between the two situations.
2. An ability to see a new problem in an old situation.
3. An ability to imagine a new function for a familiar object.
4. An ability to perceive the structure of an object.
5. An ability to recombine and transform already known modes of activity when confronted with a new problem.
6. An ability to see alternative solutions to a problem.
7. An ability to discard all trite solutions and think out an entirely new approach.

Next we propose to examine some of these features, assuming from experimental data[41] that, if it were possible to inculcate them during the years of formal education, every pupil — to a depth appropriate to individual diligence and application — should be able to develop his natural abilities to an optimum degree.

A survey of hundreds of creative-learning problems for various school subjects available in the literature demonstrates them all to be consistent with our summary in the sense that none of the problems surveyed have displayed any traits other than those listed above. Even though some of the above features, such as, for instance, the seventh, are seldom encountered in actual classroom conditions, they are not uncommon outside the classroom during, for example, mathematical and other quizzes and competitions which are arranged for schoolchildren at the regional and international levels. This is just further evidence that holding such events, even on a school or class basis, acts as a powerful stimulus to the pupils to engage in creative activity.

Some of the features listed above may seem to overlap, yet any attempt to integrate them under fewer headings only makes their coverage less exhaustive. In any event, from the educational viewpoint it appears preferable to make the list as complete as possible.

Prior to identifying the common features, it seems appropriate to provide a few illustrations of each of the seven types.

The ability to transfer knowledge and skills into new situations entirely on one's own — *the first pattern* — is a major characteristic of the creative process. Indeed, faced with a new problem, the pupil has an opportunity to apply the knowledge and skills he has already acquired. This is often quite a challenge, especially if the previously acquired knowledge does not fall within the same field as the problem to be solved.

Now for a few illustrations. In a remote locality in the tropics, workers building a steel factory put up an auxiliary structure made of brick seven metres high and five metres wide. They were then faced with a problem of moving it some distance and lowering it into a receiving pit of similar dimensions. In the absence of a crane the problem was — how to lower it home intact. After some brain-searching, someone had the idea of filling the pit with ice. The rest was easy. Labourers hauled the structure on rollers up to the pit edge and off the rollers on to the ice. As the ice melted, the structure sank until it reached the bottom, forcing out the water. In this case, only one individual proved ingenious enough to suggest using ice, i.e. the transfer of one system into another to perform a new function.

Another example. At a ceramics factory, expensive chinaware was fired on a conveyor belt in a tunnel kiln. A brick dislodged itself from the kiln lining and became jammed right in mid-ceiling projecting downwards, with the result that the chinaware was being smashed on its way through the tunnel. Removing the brick by actually getting into the tunnel was out of the question, since switching off the kiln, letting it cool down and heating it up again meant that the factory would be out of action for a long time, and the idle time would cost too much money. But what was the alternative? After some hard thinking someone suggested inviting a marksman from a nearby naval college. After several shots the brick was smashed with little damage to the chinaware.

Still another example is furnished by a happening in a big city. The local public transport authority, faced with the increasing problem of non-payment of bus fares, decided to hold monthly raffles of used-ticket numbers with prizes to be paid in kind or in currency. This proved very effective.

These three examples demonstrate *inter alia* that a transposition of knowledge may be closely — or remotely — associated depending on the relationship of the situations in hand. Thus, the ceramics factory episode is a case of close association, the construction site is an instance of remote association and the solution to the city transport problem stands somewhere midway.

Now an example of visualizing a new problem in a familiar setting — *the second pattern*. On seeing a primitive chisel dating from prehistoric times in a museum, a pupil asked the teacher: 'Does it mean prehistoric man could tell the difference between 'sharp' and 'blunt'? He must have known how to make a chisel blunt at one end and sharp at the other!' The pupil posed the problem of whether it was possible to pass judgement of prehistoric man's knowledge by the chisel he had made. The important thing about it is that the pupil entirely on his own managed to see a new problem in a routine, hum-drum setting. For our part, we must see in it a pretty complex manifestation of creativity in a perfectly spontaneous manner, whereas inculcating such useful habits in children (which, in principle, it is possible to teach to all children) in a scholastic environment involves quite an effort.

The *third pattern* in the process of creative activity is exemplified by the ability to see a new function for an existing object. An individual surrounded with the arti-facts of daily use, objects the purpose of which he knows only too well, may be able at the same time to perceive an altogether new and unexpected purpose served by an object. One person faced with the problem of driving a nail into the wall without a hammer may fail to see the possibility of using a metal ashtray. Another individual, however, does see the possibility of using the head of a drawing pin to render harmless a nail protruding through the sole of his shoe.

Just as important is an ability to see the structural side of an object — *the fourth pattern*. Faced with a situation, a problem or an unknown text, an individual may perceive either all the elements of an object indiscriminately or distinguish between what matters and what does not, at once understanding the complex of relations in which they stand with one another. For instance, one is faced with the problem of determining if there is any pattern in the number 137913151921. Those who see no more than an irregular combination of figures will never find a solution. On the other hand, those who see in it a regular combination of figures — a general principle — are likely to perceive the recurrent addition of 2 and 4.

The *fifth pattern* of the process of creative activity is that of recombining one's own familiar activities into new activities. Widely applied in virtually any field, this pattern is especially common in solving mathematical problems. For example, one is required to obtain the number 7 through carrying out operations in any combination on five twos (2, 2, 2, 2, 2). Posing this problem, as we know from experience, to any large group of pupils results in several solutions such as: 2+2+2+(2:2); (22:2)-(2+2); ([2+2]²-2):2; etc.

The *sixth pattern* of the creative process illustrates alternative reasoning, i.e. finding alternative solutions to a given problem, alternative methods of solution and confrontation of evidence, in other words, seeing a problem in all its complexity. Here is an illustration. While studying the history of the slave states which were located on what is now the territory of the USSR, seventh-formers were required to determine what was the main occupation of the population of the Bosphorus population judging by the following passage from the textbook:

In the Bosphorian kingdom, of which Panticopeus was the capital for nine centuries, the coins bore the image of a plough. On that evidence historians came to a conclusion about the main occupation of its people. Yet with new facts coming to their attention they changed their minds. What, in your opinion, was the principal occupation of the Bosphorians, taking into consideration the plough image?

While justifying their own hypotheses, the pupils came to the conclusion that the principal occupation in the Bosphorus region was either land cultivation or the forging and exporting of ploughs.

The *seventh pattern* of creativity involves contriving an altogether new approach to a problem and discarding all familiar solutions or combinations of known solutions. Typical of this pattern is proposing original solutions to problems. Another two examples are cited below to illustrate this creative approach in its multiple manifestations. Take the problem of plotting four equilateral triangles using three or six matchsticks. The problem is popular with schoolchildren and university graduates. It can only be solved if the candidate discards the habitual psychological image of a two-dimensional triangle. Once an alternative approach involving three-dimensional triangles has been advanced the problem is quickly solved. In this way the candidate shows himself capable of not only seeing a problem but also of devising a new method of solving it.

Another example. In a history lesson, sixth-formers were given a problem to solve:

'In 843, under the Treaty of Verdun the Empire of Charlemagne was partitioned between his heirs, who were the sons of Louis, his elder son. Would the empire have collapsed if Charlemagne had had only one heir?' The pupils answered that the Carolingean Empire disintegrated not because of the number of heirs but because of the development of feudalism, an answer demonstrating that they were capable of transposing previously acquired knowledge into a situation altogether new to them.

In solving a particular problem creative behaviour patterns cannot be expected to manifest themselves spontaneously but arise each time in various combinations and to varying degrees. This depends upon the content drawn from social experience — which is also an element of curriculum content.

These creative behaviour patterns are of a special nature in the sense that this activity is not predictable in hard and fast terms, neither can it be divided into a finite number of operations in advance. It is not possible either to predict the type, character and complexity of problems that have yet to arise, let alone solutions to these problems. The above patterns cannot be very well described in strict detail, and the best one can do is to give the reader a general idea about them by way of example. The acquisition of these patterns, as well as the actual experience of creative activity itself, is only possible through the search for solutions to new problems, a search involving the transposition, recombination and transformation of methods, the ability to see the essence of problems, etc. One cannot impose any universal recipe for this kind of operation, since it must lend itself to solving new problems and therefore cannot be conceived in advance on the basis of past experience. Experience in creative activity is as specific as the individual engaged in it, yet it is still possible to trace common patterns. Creative activity can be interpreted as a process whereby man, whether objectively or subjectively, creates new things by following specific intellectual patterns that defy any precise description in terms of a controlled system of operations or actions. This definition appears especially valuable for educators concerned with creative activities that are hardly likely to yield any new quality which is of use to society. At the same time, a new quality by no means always results from subjective creative activity (accidental archeological or geological finds for example). Yet, without instruction, creative activity as a process simply cannot be imagined. However, our interest focuses on a particular characteristic of creative activity, a special element of social experience differing in content from the first two elements of that experience, i.e. from knowledge of and experience in how to use and reproduce familiar methods. One may be familiar with several methods and know how to apply them, yet this is not enough to enable a search for solutions to new problems. Experience in this kind of search differs in principle from the content of the first two elements to comprise a third element of social experience. It has a special function to perform other than that of merely reproducing already accumulated culture — a function of developing it further, of creating new cultural values, something that is unattainable with only the first two elements at one's disposal.

5. THE PLACE OF EMOTIONAL ATTITUDES

Man's needs derive not only from his biological but also from his social background. Man's needs and emotions as a component of culture are socially-generated needs and emotions: needs for learning, including non-motivated learning, the need for communication, the need for mutual sympathy and co-operation, material needs. In short, all needs in their entirety (subject to additions and modifications with the expansion and enrichment of social experience) comprise a unique and essential prerequisite to social development[42]. Emotional education is a special contribution of social experience to the content and quality of an educated personality. Despite the links between all elements (on which we propose to dwell later), the content of *the fourth element*, including standards for *an emotionally mature attitude to reality*, differs from the content of the first three elements, as does its function in the replication and development of culture. Its function is to guide moral, aesthetic and emotional stimuli, needs and ideals, i.e. all the manifestations of an attitude to reality, activity and the products of activity. Man's needs (and the emotional sphere derived from these needs) are responsible for his selective attitude to reality and activity.

The content of standards for emotional education is specific in that it consists not of knowledge or skills but of emotionally mature attitudes to reality and activity. The sphere of man's attitude to his environment, i.e. the sphere of emotions, is neither identical with the content of his knowledge of the above activity nor with that of his skills and habits. This is a domain apart. Emotions have three independent parametres: quality (joy, sorrow, etc.), degree and object. An individual may be familiar with the standards of behaviour and even keep within them, but at the same time may adopt an indifferent or negative view of them. In such a case a person should not be considered as emotionally mature or even well taught in the context of emotional education. Someone may be familiar with an ideology and may even know how to explain certain phenomena on the basis of this ideology, yet he may not be convinced of its validity; it may fail to evoke an emotional response in him. Creating one's own ideology means not merely that one is familiar with it but, indeed, is convinced of its validity. In short, it is assumed to be one's code of conduct, finding expression in patterns of behaviour and activity, patterns which assume a natural and spontaneous form in the material and intellectual domains.

A team of Moscow psychologists staged an experiment on a group of pre-schoolers who, being aware of standards of good behaviour, did not behave as they had been taught because that way they had more fun. It is only after the opposite, i.e. desirable, emotional pattern prevailed that their behaviour was in accordance with the standards they had acquired.

Emotions always have content and are a form of reflecting reality, but a special form differing, for instance, from logical reasoning. It is in that sense that Pestalozzi remarked: 'Before lecturing them on a virtue, I try to evoke in children its living, emotional image'[43]. Emotions border on the realm of the subconscious, beyond reason's control. Emotions which are subject to being inculcated in the younger generation should not be identified with reasoning, the latter presupposing a certain quantity and systematization of knowledge. Emotions comprise a special content of activity and originate in social development. The quality and intensity of emotions increase as the area of reality within their reach expands. Thus, man's aesthetic attitude towards nature is not supposed to be innate. It is rather a product of historical development.

An emotionally mature frame of mind does not automatically follow from the material content designed to inculcate it. The same kind of activity evokes different emotions which sometimes clash in different individuals, as well as in the same individual under different circumstances. Ambivalent emotions (pleasure/regret, etc.) may have one and the same effect. Emotion is destructive of thought; the former retains its independence of the latter. One emotion may suppress another, even though the motivation behind the suppressed emotion may be stronger and be regarded by the emotion-bearer as more valid. Fear may suppress an action prompted by reason.

Emotion is always an experience and, being a facet of consciousness and a form to reflect reality, is always different from cognitive processes. The relative independence of emotions from the other forms in which human activity manifests itself (such as the intellectual form) invariably and promptly affects (sometimes in a tempestuous manner) physiological processes and metabolism, whereas perception and reasoning 'have no or little bearing on biological processes'[44]. Emotional experiences are counted in dozens (surprise, sorrow, satisfaction, etc.), each one obviously different from the others. It appears just as easy to distinguish between the degrees of emotional response irrespective of the objects which provoked the reaction.

The relative aloofness of the emotional sphere is additionally borne out by the fact that emotionally-generated motivation selects from outside only that information which is in agreement with its motives, this information not always being consistent.

The following conclusions of a United States author[45] seem relevant to the present discourse. Referring to facial expression as a language of emotions understandable, in Charles Darwin's opinion, to all (excepting psychically anomalous individuals, according to clinical research data), the author argues that facial expression has its origins in cultural evolution. Facial expression has become a means, according to the author, of social signalization about inner motivations and conditions. However, neither facial expression nor the emotion behind it are necessarily an expression of the meaning of the accompanying speech and thought. Indeed, facial expression may contradict verbal expression. The author lists among essential emotions pleasure, interest, distress, disgust, anger, disdain, surprise, shame, fear. Each of them manifests itself to a different degree, performs an important role in personality functioning and therefore is important in moulding personality. A lack of emotional education and, notably, its introspective aspects may lead to a shortcoming in the ability to share other people's emotions. Thus, a person without a sense of shame is likely to develop a lack of self-respect, etc. The entire language of emotions, the vocabulary of facial expression is handed down from one generation to another. In an introduction to the same source[46], Simonov analyses all the above emotions into three groups according to the human needs the emotions are supposed to satisfy. Thus, the need for self-preservation is accompanied by such emotions as surprise, disgust and fear; the need for communication or 'belonging' is associated with anger, disdain, shame, distress (sorrow); the need for learning with interest, pleasure (boredom).

In each epoch, these purely human or humanized needs and the emotions they evoke, have their own historical origin and hence are associated with all the circumstances of that origin. Yet these emotions may manifest themselves independently of circumstances and gain, as it were, their independence, especially in personality traits. The relative independence of the content of emotional activity is additionally corroborated by man's ability to evoke in his own self the emotions he believes to be important or desirable.

The historical nature of emotional experience has been convincingly demonstrated by Dodonov[47] who sought to base his classification of emotions on socio-psychological rather than on psycho-physiological findings. He analyses emotions into the following types: altruistic, communicative, gloristic (pride), the emotions of activity and success, aggression, romantic, gnostic, aesthetic, hedonistic, acquisitive. Many of the above types of emotions (altruistic, gloristic, aesthetic, hedonistic) have evolved with the evolution of mankind, others have been enriched and deepened in the course of that evolution. The analysis of emotions into types has also made it abundantly clear that different individuals, depending on their background, are capable of different emotions to a different degree [48]. If one is brought up in emotionally impoverished conditions, it will inevitably affect the emotional perception as a whole[49]. Therefore, education involves not only imparting knowledge, skills and creative activity but also broadening and enriching the pupils' emotional sphere.

6. INTERDEPENDENCE OF THE ELEMENTS OF CURRICULUM CONTENT

The content of social experience may thus be broadly analysed into four elements: (1) knowledge of reality, i.e. of nature, society, technology and methods of activity; (2) experience in using activity, i.e. skills and useful habits; (3) experience in creative activity involving a readiness to confront new problems; (4) experience of an emotional attitude to one's environment and to one another.

All the above elements in each epoch possess specific content and pattern depending on the particular cultural level, prevailing social system and the classes comprising it. In describing the composition of culture and social experience one should be aware that each of these elements differs depending on the historical epoch and on the prevailing social system of that epoch.

The elements are interconnected in more ways than one. Each element of social experience is essential to the functioning of the other elements. Thus, without knowledge it is impossible either to reproduce activity or to apply it creatively. The very search for new methods of activity is concomitant with the replication of familiar methods. The second and third elements always embody knowledge to serve as a means of action and a guide in performing it, while they also serve to produce new knowledge or reproduce and fix knowledge. The first three elements of social experience always presuppose a definite attitude, since any activity is brought about by a demand for such activity, while an attitude (no matter what) arising therein invariably has a content of its own.

It is absolutely essential that all the elements of social experience become part of the content of general education, otherwise some of these elements will not be transmitted to the younger generation to the detriment of the replication and further development of culture. Even though the presence of all these elements in curriculum content is inevitable anyway, they are not necessarily transmitted to an equal degree to all social strata in each generation.

The above four elements of curriculum content also produce feedback. The acquisition of a logically consecutive element is bound to affect the quality or degree of acquisition of a logically preceding element. Thus, the acquisition of the latter element embodied in skills and useful habits affects the acquisition of knowledge at the level of application in familiar situations, making it more effective and useful. The acquisition of experience in a creative activity means the acquisition of knowledge and skills at the level of their application. Through their acquisition, knowledge and skills become useful and flexible, while the acquirer develops a capability either to use knowledge in a condensed state or, if the need should arise, to unfold that knowledge to the full. The emotionally mature attitude enables the acquired skills to be consolidated and knowledge to be committed to memory, thereby raising the efficiency of consolidated acquisition per unit of time.

Any coherent record of knowledge, whether written or verbal, contains not only information but also the potential, expressed or implied, for that information to be used in hitherto unknown situations, as well as to evoke in the reader or listener an attitude. In short, any text may be claimed to contain all the four elements of social experience, though this is not always obvious. Any text containing a definite piece of information reflects a definite piece of learned reality. Its cognition has always been aimed at satisfying a particular human need, attained by methods appropriate to the case. The analysis of any text is consequently bound to identify all the above elements of social experience in which the given text has origins. The acquisition of a text presupposes the acquisition of the information it contains, a familiarization with the fields and methods of reproductive and creative application of that information and the existence of demand for this acquisition activity. This is just another proof of the actual existence of the above elements of social experience and the links between them.

Despite these links, it is not altogether irrational to divide social experience into elements — not only because the analyst perceives in abstract terms differences between them, but also because in reality each of the elements may have an independent existence. Thus, there is a piece of knowledge for which the field of application remains for a time unknown, just as there is a piece of knowledge about active methods in the absence of the skills to use these methods; there are active methods to reproduce familiar methods and their outcomes without any alterations; there are active methods (skills) spontaneously acquired by children without understanding their procedures; and finally, there is a creative-search activity which may be either altogether new or may radically transform already known methods of activity. The content of emotional education or of an emotionally mature attitude to reality may differ for the same activity, i.e. activity as such does not always evoke the same attitude. Emotions are relatively independent of the intellectual and physical activity they have a potential bearing upon.

One argument in favour of analysing content into the above elements is the fact that using an active method has its own content. Likewise, creativity can be interpreted in terms of using knowledge and activity patterns, yet the former is not reducible to the latter. The existence and use of these two types of activity, each having quite different contents, do not yet involve creativity. For that, there is a need for yet another activity and that means another content.

An emotion also possesses content, as long as it plays the role of an activity for evaluating the environment and oneself in that environment. The emotions of joy and sorrow, pleasure and regret, etc., also have an evaluative function. The first three elements of activity content, however, do not provide emotional activity with the same content.

Each preceding element of content substantiates each following element, providing it with content, but only to a certain extent. Each following element of activity content modifies the nature and quality of each preceding element, and incorporates and integrates these modifications. All this is illustrative of both the relative independence of each content element and its links with other elements.

It follows from the above that social experience is a system of elements, each with a content of its own and with a function of reproducing and developing culture and society as a whole, a function not interchangeable with functions of the other elements. The elements of social experience are ever present in culture, irrespective of the epoch, even though each of the elements may change in quantity of content from one epoch to the next. In the absence of any of the elements and thus in the absence of its respective content, the replication and development of culture, and hence society as a whole, would be unthinkable.

Let us conclude with a few more words about the function of each element being different from that of any of the other elements. Knowledge has a function of providing an image of reality, of conditions in which to take bearings in this reality and to serve as a guide in the attainment of goals. Experience in using skills has a function of replicating culture by following the patterns of activity hitherto accumulated. This replication, as far as quantity is concerned, is expandable to involve, for example, an ever-greater output of machine-tools, cultivated land, textbooks, housing units, etc.

Experience in creative activity has a function of purposefully transforming the environment to a new qualitative level, i.e. of further developing society in all its aspects.

Experience in emotional attitudes towards reality provides a basis for determining an individual attitude towards reality, establishing a ratio between the environment and one's activity within this environment, on the one hand, and one's needs and motivations on the other.

At this stage of the discourse we are trying to justify the division of social, and hence cultural, experience into separate elements. As good a basis for such a division as any appears to be the characteristics of content and functions of each of the elements in the activity of society and each member of society. Indeed, the third element, i.e. experience in creativity, even though remaining indispensable for the development of society as a whole, is neither always nor fully available to every member of society. The second element, i.e. the replication of skills on which hinges the existence of society, does not invariably involve the application of knowledge known to society. Activities can be reproduced as manual skills with no actual understanding of the principles behind the activity, in other words, without knowledge. Knowledge itself can exist completely apart from the methods for using it and give no idea at all about its own application, even though knowledge is a primary requisite to perform an activity and enables reality to be viewed in broader outlines. Because of their interconnections, these elements differ not only in their functions but also in the employment of their functions.

The grounds given for dividing social experience into elements can be expanded still further by adding the argument of the relative independence and incompatibility of the functions performed by these elements in educating and enlightening the younger generation and every member of society with a view to preserving the content of culture amassed by that society. If one of these elements is passed on to the younger generation to the exclusion of all the others, it cannot be expected to perform its functions and, vice versa, not one of the elements can be replaced by a combination of the remaining three. Each performs an indispensable function. Knowledge of the methods of an activity is not equivalent to experience in applying these methods and this is particularly true of creativity. The reproduction of actions contributes neither to knowledge of the actions nor to the development of creative potential. It would be obviously unrealistic to expect schoolchildren to acquire entirely on their own all the knowledge and skills accumulated by society, no matter how much effort the children make. It would be an impossible feat even within the limits of one school subject. Likewise, the mere imparting of knowledge and the associated skills without regard for the learner's emotional side cannot give him an education worthy of that name.

It will be recalled that the same four elements recur in each act of purposive activity, since that act presupposes knowledge of the method of such activity, the skill of using this method, the ability to transform it if necessary and, last but not least, an attitude to that act.

This examination of the structure of social experience seeks to identify those elements of curriculum content which are essential to moulding a comprehensively developed personality, i.e. to making social experience available for the younger generation as a whole and for each normal representative of that generation. With this purpose in view, there is a need to superimpose the composition of social experience as a whole on the composition of curriculum content imparted to every schoolchild. Indeed, the personality traits acquired through formal education result from the acquisition of curriculum content. Since the goal of education is to mould a generation capable of replicating and further developing the cultural heritage and social experience accumulated by society, the structure of curriculum content should be aligned with the structure of cultural content. There is nothing outside culture that is relevant for inclusion in curriculum content, since curriculum content should not have in it anything that has not been created by society through its socio-historical evolution. Each trait of an individual as a social being is the result and embodiment of acquired culture. Thus, knowledge, skills, abilities, morals, ideals, willpower and motivations have arisen through social development, through gradually accumulated culture. It is personality that plays the role of a cultural bearer. In composition and structure curriculum content should not differ from social experience as a whole. The structure of curriculum content should be compatible with that of social experience in order to achieve a comprehensively developed personality. 'Should be' compatible, not 'is' compatible, since both the findings of theoretical didactics and the practice of formal education are indicative of ignoring in some cases some elements of content such as, for example, the need to encourage creative activity. Inattention to all the elements of content also results in a tendency to overlook emotional education in published research. A clear vision of teaching objectives combined with an educational insight are the essentials for successful scholastic performance. The side effects of a narrow-minded approach to the composition of curriculum content include: a prevalence of hanging on to rote teaching; and a lack of creative assignments in the class in the absence of any coherent system of assignments in the textbooks.

A democratic society based on humanism should be concerned with and capable of imparting to the younger generation all the structural elements of social experience in a manner appropriate to the pupils' capacity. The content of education in such a society can be defined as a humanistically-oriented and educationally-adapted system of knowledge, skills, experience in creative activity and experience in emotionally mature attitudes to reality and activity, a system the content of which, if and when acquired, should favour the development of a comprehensively developed personality equipped to contribute to the replication and further development of a modern, progressive culture.

It already appears appropriate to derive certain conclusions from the above formula, which hopefully should benefit not only theoretical didactics but also scholastic performance.

Our four elements are contained in both curriculum content in general and subject content in particular. As a rule, all these elements should be present in the content of each study unit.

As far as the organization of teaching is concerned, the above analysis of social experience, and hence curriculum content, favours the identification of not only a system of knowledge but also a system of *skills and useful habits*, i.e. of those methods of activity the reproduction of which — upon receiving appropriate information — enables their mastery. A system developed after this pattern for each school subject should make up an integral whole to serve as a core to secondary education. A system of intellectual procedures and practical skills should be included in the curriculum on an equal footing with theory and, on being adequately reflected in the content and structure of textbooks, should become an integral part of practical schooling.

It appears essential, within the content of each particular subject, to specify the *creative element* and to arrange it in a definite system, so that the scope and means for this content to be imparted to the pupils are determined. At some future stage, this content is expected to become an obligatory component of curriculum which — on being embodied in textbooks and other instructional materials — will actually comprise the core curriculum.

Let us now examine the background to forming *emotional attitudes*. Emotional training, which forms part of education in its own right, becomes, by virtue of the specifics of teaching, at least partly a product of all the other components, since there can be no educational act without an influence (positive or negative) on socialization. Besides, an emotional response is material, i.e. oriented on a particular content. Hence there is a problem of proposing a curriculum which would cover instruction and socialization, and also would develop the socialization potential of each school subject. This is a problem requiring a prolonged and detailed study.

In stressing the links between the elements of content, one simply cannot ignore the extent to which the compilers of curricula and textbooks understand school subjects and teaching material. This also concerns the schoolteachers, the more so as instruction is a deliberately and purposefully organized process. If all the teacher does is to organize a particular activity for the pupils within strictly defined limits, the end product is bound to be monotonous. If a teacher simply presents a verbal discourse of second-hand knowledge which only requires memorization, the result will be superficial. If a teacher trains the pupils to blindly follow a pattern, the pupils will get into the habit of reproducing activities strictly after that pattern. Any positive results will be due to a deviation on the part of the pupils themselves. Thus, to break the monotony of instruction, a whole variety of activities must be organized for the pupils in agreement with the object and purpose of the various elements of the curriculum.

So far we have advanced the most essential and practical conclusions based on a theoretical analysis of curriculum content. The theoretical as well as practical effects upon the content of education of the ideas presented earlier in this book will be dealt with in more detail in the chapter that follows.

REFERENCES

1. Žurakovskij, G.E. Očerki po istorii antičnoj pedagogiki. Izd. 2-e. Moskva, Izdatel'stvo Akademii pedagogičeskih nauk RSFSR, 1963, p. 198.
2. Davydov, V.V. Sootnošenie ponjatij 'formirovanie' i 'razvitie' psihiki. In: Menčinskaja, N.A., et al. Obučenie i razvitie. Moskva, 'Prosveščenie', 1966, p. 38.
3. Leont'ev, A.N. Problemy razvitija psihiki. Izd. 2-e. Moskva, Mysl', 1965, p. 358.
4. Česnokov, D.I. Istoričeskij materializm. 1965, p. 389.
5. Mežuev, V.M. O ponjatii kultury. Učebnye zapiski Moskovskogo gosudarstvennogo instituta kultury (Moskva), vyp. 14, 1967, p. 26.
6. Staerman, E.M. Problemy kultury v zapadnoj sociologii. Voprosy filosofii (Moskva), no. 1, 1967.
7. Kopnin, P.V. Logičeskie osnovy nauki. Kiev, 1968, p. 16.
8. Itel'son, L.B. Lekcii po obščej psihologii. Vladimir, Vladimirskij pedagogičeskij institut im. P.I. Lebedeva-Poljanskogo, 1970, p. 223-224, p. 215-216.
9. Spasskij, B.I. Istorija fiziki. T.1. Moskva, 1963, p. 192-194.
10. Piaže, Ž. [Piaget, J.] Kak deti obrazovyvajut matematičeskie ponjatija. Voprosy psihologii (Moskva), no. 4, 1966, p. 121.
11. Gal'perin, I.Ja.; El'konin, D.B. K analizy teorii Ž. Piaže o razvitii detskogo myslenija. In: Flejven, D.H. Genetičeskaja psihologija Žaka Piaže. Moskva, 1967, p. 606-607.
12. Rubinštejn, S.L. Problema sposobnostej i voprosy psihologičeskoj teorii. Voprosy psihologii (Moskva), no. 3, 1960, p. 13.
13. Taylor, C.W., ed. Creativity: progress and potential. New York, McGraw Hill, 1964.
14. Anderson, H.H. Creativity and its cultivation. New York, Harper & Row, 1959.
15. Spearman, C. Creative mind. London, 1930, p. 55.
16. Berlyne, D.E. Structure and direction in thinking. New York, Wiley, 1965.
17. Taylor, C.W.; Barron, F., eds. Scientific activity: its recognition and development. New York, Wiley, 1963.

18. Taylor, C.W.; Ghiselin, B.; Smith, W.R. The creativity and other contributions of one sample of research scientists. *In*: Taylor, C.W.; Barron, F., eds. *Scientific creativity: its recognition and development.* New York, Wiley, 1963, p. 70.
19. Guilbert, H.E.; Tevelle; Wertheimer, M., eds. *Contemporary approaches to creative thinking.* New York, 1963.
20. Samarin, Ju.A. *Očerki psihologii uma: osobennosti umstvennoj dejatel'nosti škol'nikov.* Moskva, Izdatel'stvo Akademii pedagogičeskih nauk RSFSR, 1962, p. 484.
21. Gurova, L.L. *Psihologičeskij analiz rešenija zadač.* Voronež, Izdatel'stvo Voronežskogo universiteta, 1976. 327 p.
22. Lejtes, N.S. Sklonnost' k trudy kak faktor odarennosti. *Izvestija Akademii pedagogičeskih nauk RSFSR* (Moskva), vyp. 25, 1950.
23. Šorohova, E.V., ed. *Issledovanija myšlenija v sovetskoj psihologii.* Moskva, 'Nauka', 1966.
24. Bernštejn, M.S. Psihologija naučnogo tvorčestva. *Voprosy psihologii* (Moskva), no. 3, 1965, p. 156-164.
25. Bernštejn, M.S. O prirode naučnogo tvorčestva. *Voprosy psihologii* (Moskva), no. 6, 1966.
26. Ponomarev, P.Ja. *Psihologija tvorčestva.* Moskva, 1976.
27. Ponomarev, P.Ja. *Znanija, myšlenie i umstvennoe razvitie.* Moskva, 'Prosveščenie', 1967. 264 p.
28. Ponomarev, P.Ja. *Psihologija tvorčestva i pedagogika.* Moskva, 1976.
29. Al'tšuller, R.S. *Algoritm izobretenija.* Moskva, 1973.
30. Mikulinskij, S.R.; Jaroševskij, M.G., eds. *Naučnoe tvorčestvo.* Moskva, 'Nauka', 1969. 446 p.
31. Puškin, V.N. *Evristika: nauka o tvorčeskom myšlenii.* Moskva, Politizdat, 1967. 271 p.
32. Matjuškin, A.M., ed. *Psihologija myšlenija: sbornik perevodov s nemeckogo i anglijskogo.* Moskva, 'Progress', 1965. 533 p.
33. Šorohova, E.V., ed. *Osnovye napravlenija issledovanij psihologii myšlenija v kapitalističeskih stranah.* Moskva, 'Nauka', 1966. 299 p.
34. Davydova, G.A. *Tvorčestvo i dialektika.* Moskva, 1975.
35. Jaroševskij, M.G., ed. *Problemy naučnogo tvorčestva v sovremennoj psihologii.* Moskva, 'Nauka', 1971. 334 p.
36. Kočergin, A.N. *Modelirovanie myšlenija.* Moskva, 1969.
37. Matjuškin, A.M. *Problemy situacii v myšlenii i obučenii.* Moskva, 1967.
38. Parnes, S. *Guide-book for creative thinking.* New York, 1963.
39. Kozielecki, J. *Rozwiazywanie problemóv.* Warszawa, 1969.
40. Pietrasinski, L. *Myślenie twórcze.* Warszawa, 1969.
41. Lerner, I.Ja., ed. *Poznavatel'nye zadači v obučenii gumanitarnym naukam.* Moskva, 'Pedagogika', 1972. 239 p.
42. Simonov, P.V. *Vysšaja nervnaja dejatel'nost' čeloveka: motivacionno-emocional'nye aspekty.* Moskva, 1975.
43. Pestalocci, G. *Izbrannye pedagogičeskie proizvedenija.* Moskva, Izdatel'stvo Akademii pedagogičeskih nauk RSFSR, 1961, t.2, p. 147.
44. Šingarev, G.H. *Emocii i čuvstva.* Moskva, 1971, p. 5.
45. Izard, K.I. Emocional'nyj kontakt. *Nauka i žizn'* (Moskva), no. 12, 1977.
46. Ibid.
47. Dodonov, B.I. *Emocija kak cennost'.* Moskva, 1978, p. 77.
48. Ol'sannikova, A.E.; Rabinovič, L.A. Opyt issledovanija nekotoryh individual'nyh harakteristik emocional'nosti. *Voprosy psihologii* (Moskva), no. 3, 1974, p. 67.
49. Gel'gorn, E.; Luffbaraun, Dž. *Emocii i emocional'nye rasstrojstva.* Moskva, 1966, p. 312.

CHAPTER III
Foundations for constructing curriculum content

1. CURRICULUM CONSTRUCTION IN EDUCATIONAL PLANNING

As stated in Chapter I, the particular domain of interest for didactics, as far as the theory of curriculum content goes, is to contribute to the construction of that content. The role of didactics in this case is not simply to provide an account of a process actually taking place. It must prescribe *how* to construct that content.

Since, in the view of didactics, curriculum content is inseparable from the activity of teaching, the construction of that content should be considered as a component of educational planning in general. Nowadays, educational planning is an important branch of activity. This activity actually governs the development of a *normative sphere* in education which, in broad outline, can be interpreted as all the elements of knowledge whose interconnections to a varying degree embrace educational principles and rules, methods and techniques embodied in research papers, curricula, recommendations, textbooks, etc. We are going to examine the levels of the normative sphere in which education is the object of scientifically substantiated planning.

One can set out to define this normative sphere by visualizing in broad theoretical outlines how to carry out teaching on a *normative model* of instruction, which is the first step on the way from the theoretical definition of instruction to its actual introduction in the scholastic environment (see Section 2, Chapter I). At this stage of definition one deals with such educational terms as the content, principles and methods of education.

The next step is to designate *the broad theoretical guidelines for the teaching of each school subject* (likewise in normative terms).

The consolidation of these broad concepts should begin with the planning of syllabuses. A syllabus is a standardized design for the teaching of a particular school subject reflected in its curriculum and guidelines for the teacher and pupils. Proceeding from the existing general definitions of curriculum, one may safely claim it to be the collection of syllabuses corresponding in number to the total number of school subjects. Thus, Hirst and Peters take the term 'curriculum' to be the 'label for a programme or course of activities which is explicitly organized as the means whereby pupils may attain the desired objectives, whatever these may be'[1].

One can get a clear idea about the content and process of the teaching in the *descriptions of syllabuses* which one commonly finds in surveys on particular subjects.

And finally, our understanding of teaching activity is taking on quite definite shape and we can now place at the teacher's disposal not merely a complete set of norms but a *means* of conducting that activity. In this perspective, a *syllabus* is the final stage in unfolding educational principles, in consolidating them at the level of a particular subject and making them teachable (leaving any further planning of content to the teacher's discretion).

A syllabus and the subject course in which it assumes its final form are indispensable in teaching. This is demonstrated by the dual function of a subject course as a final blueprint for instruction. A subject course can be defined as a set of theoretical and material means to teach a particular subject. It takes the following forms: (a) actual content and guidelines concerning the techniques and structure of teaching in a particular subject in particular conditions for a particular purpose; (b) textbooks, visual aids and instructional technology. All this is presented graphically in Table 1.

TABLE 1. Planning instruction.

Levels of the normative sphere	*Embodied in*
1. Normative model of teaching	Literature of theoretical didactics
2. Normative model of teaching each particular school subject	Theoretical reports on teaching school subjects
3. Syllabus	Curriculum — general guidelines
4. Subject course	Actual content and guidelines concerning the techniques and structure of teaching in a particular subject: textbooks, visual aids and educational technology.

The principle of structural integrity for curriculum content is based on the following didactic principle: *in identifying an element of subject content it is necessary to take into account all the other elements.*

Thus, in identifying a system of reading skills for the content of literature, the following principles should be taken into account: (a) the system of theoretical knowledge (the academic and historic appreciation of literature involving systems of criteria; appreciation of the characteristics of fiction and poetry and of their development; appreciation of aesthetics, ethics, history, etc.); (b) the system of values that this subject is expected to inculcate (appraisal of the author's ideas; aesthetic approach to the literary work and to reality in general; literary and aesthetic taste; aesthetic ideal); (c) the characteristics of creative activity[5].

Once the system of reading skills have been identified, it becomes itself a didactic principle enabling the rationalization and systematization of the set of skills within the limits of the school subject of literature. To identify the skills comprising the above set, one may also resort to non-didactic principles such as those of psychology for example. Thus, by using as a psychological principle those difficulties which the pupils encounter in learning, one may identify the corresponding types of skills the mastery of which makes learning easier, enabling the identification or selection of the principal learning action, confirming and demonstrating the correct solutions, pinpointing errors and inexactitudes, etc.[6].

The linkages between didactic rationales manifest themselves to a varying degree throughout the three levels of curriculum construction. Accordingly, they are analysed into the rationales of: (a) theoretical definition; (b) syllabus construction; (c) compilation of the lesson. The problem of scientific sources of curriculum construction at each of the levels was examined in general in Chapter I. Didactic-related points therein are studied in the following sections.

The theoretical definition of curriculum content is based on such didactic rationales as: familiarity with the construction of didactic theory; familiarity with a particular objective of didactics; familiarity with the scientific methodology of teaching; knowing how to apply a systems approach to didactic research; and knowing how to interpret social demands in an educational context. The source of this knowledge is research reports on didactic methodology. At this level of definition, didactic rationales indicate the need to consider different levels of curriculum construction, to define the general goals of education as elements of curriculum content and also the need to bear in mind from the beginning the linkages between and within subjects, i.e. those which are to result from content construction at the subsequent levels.

These guidelines are adapted to suit each school subject and complemented with knowledge of a normative character concerning its definition, a definition prompted by the assumed involvement of subject content in teaching activity, by the role of that subject in general education, and by the knowledge, activity methods and creative-activity content of that subject. At this level, didactic rationales serve to substantiate the theoretical definition of curriculum content and its expression at the level of the school subject.

As guidelines for the construction of curriculum content, these rationales should enable, for instance, the following question to be answered: what criteria should be used in moving from the general concept of modes of activity as elements in curriculum content to the identification of skills and habits common to all subjects? One principle may be to identify those things which do not change for any particular school subject. The inventory of modes of activity obtained so far should be examined for a particular subject. The main principle of this examination is the inventory itself. If, for instance, the existing curricula and textbooks fail to make full use of the modes of activity which have been listed, there is a need to add the missing elements. On the other hand, if an element is duplicated in several subjects or certain skills not on the inventory are still found in certain subjects, it may be expedient to delete an element or two in order to make the subject (the curricula and textbooks) less dense.

But this may lead to other problems and it may be necessary to resort to principles outside the domain of didactics which, in this particular instance, will more often than not be psychological. For all that, it is didactic guidelines which direct this activity. And this applies to the subsequent level of study materials. Any further expression of activities will result in a situation where the inventory of specific skills and habits for each school subject becomes a didactic rationale for a process of compiling texts and assignments oriented to developing these skills and habits in the pupils. It will be recalled that the general guidelines identified at the first level remain a norm for the activity of curriculum construction at the subsequent levels. Thus, in compiling study materials, one should take into account the whole context of the instructional process as well as the characteristics of both learning and teaching.

As was stated earlier in this book, the level of study material is the ultimate level of the normative sphere. This is the level immediately preceding practice, the penultimate stage prior to introducing a project through actual teaching. And the ultimate level is that component of the teacher's activity which Kuzmina calls constructive activity, assuming that the teacher himself designs the content of his lesson and establishes the order of priorities for himself and his pupils[7].

An idea of the relationship of levels in the normative sphere and of the influences on curriculum content at every level may provide a criterion for a variety of activities both in the field of theoretical definition as well as in that of educational planning. Thus, 'Prosveščenie' Publishers, the biggest producer of textbooks, teaching aids and manuals in the USSR, has adopted this approach as a basis for its system of textbook publishing[8].

2. DETERMINANTS OF CURRICULUM CONSTRUCTION

Factors, sources and principles. In Chapter II, the four elements of social experience and curriculum content were examined in terms of education in general without examining the content of curricula and textbooks in detail. These four elements provide a basis for a theoretical foundation for the all-round development and socialization of the personality. This is not, however, adequate to guide the selection of curriculum content from social experience in the sense of those essential components to attain the goals of education. There is an obvious need for further clarification, since, throughout the world, the compilation of curricula and their subsequent appearance in textbook form only provides further evidence of the lack of properly corroborated criteria.

What are, for instance, the essential aspects of the natural sciences which should be learned in the complete course of general education? Is it really indispensable, for example, to include the formula of a lens — which seems to be virtually omnipresent?

The usual practice is to solve such dilemmas pragmatically, by working with an expert or relying on the common sense and often subjective views of curriculum compilers. More often than not, the end result is a top-heavy curriculum which, once its unsuitability to the pupils' abilities becomes evident, is subject to drastic revision — only to fall into the opposite extreme. If curriculum content falls short of complete coverage, it is probably due to a lack of educational awareness on the part of the compilers or to the absence of adequate criteria to select teaching material which covered all the elements.

These levels correspond exactly to the levels of curriculum content identified earlier. The general theoretical concept of curriculum content (as well as the corresponding teaching methods) is a component of the normative model of teaching. The content of a school subject is a component of the concept of teaching this subject embodied in the appropriate syllabus. And, finally, the study material is a component of the subject course. This is how the construction of curriculum content becomes a component of educational planning.

The construction of planned content is a *professional activity in its own right* which is performed by educationists, curriculum planners and textbook compilers. And they are naturally expected to concentrate on what has a direct bearing on teaching activity and, first and foremost, on the underlying principles. On the other hand, they themselves are in need of scientifically substantiated norms to guide their specific contribution to educational planning. These norms are to be considered during their activity of planning curriculum content.

The activity of establishing these prescriptions is in itself normative, since it should provide a basis for the development of more detailed specifications. In this context, the above statement is a normative model for *the construction of curriculum content* at all levels.

On the basis of the above concept, basic ways of planning curriculum content are presented below:

1. *Theoretical activity of a didactic nature*: the definition of levels and sources for curriculum construction;
2. *Theoretical activity at the level of teaching a particular subject*: the designation of the functions of a given subject and methods of presenting the composition of a curriculum in this subject in accordance with its functions;
3. *The search for didactic principles* on which to base the construction of curricula at the levels of theoretical definition, the actual school subject and study materials;
4. *The actual process of creating curriculum content.*

In the following section we intend to examine each of the above activities in turn.

The definition of levels and sources for curriculum construction derives from a systems approach and the resulting hierarchy of levels. In Chapter I we proposed and evaluated a concept for the content of general education based on social goals.

Certain elements of this model already exist and are recorded in theoretical studies on didactics and the methodology of teaching for particular subjects, in textbooks and manuals, workbooks, etc. Cases where the material is considered inadequate or where there are shortcomings in curriculum content are due to inconsistencies in the logic of teaching a particular subject, or failure to take note of psychological research, etc. Yet the most common cause of substandard performance is the failure to adopt an integrated approach to curriculum content, a failure that can only be rectified by planning based on didactic lines. A suitable approach is readily attainable through ordering and defining the didactic and methodological categories according to an integrated structure.

An important stage in constructing curriculum content is represented by *the definition of the functions of a particular school subject,* functions which are determined by the role the subject performs in attaining the general goals of education and which, in their turn, determine the composition and structure of its content. It is by examining these functions that one identifies the relative share of each element in curriculum composition for the given subject, the nature of connections between elements and the most important element in the context of that particular subject.

The principal task for didactic research with reference to curricula consists of furnishing *didactic rationales for their compilation.* The term 'didactic rationales' stands for *a set of norms serving to regulate the selection of important educational elements in social experience.* These norms are nothing more than principles, whether primary or secondary in order of priority, which are typically derived exclusively from the content of the science of didactics. In determining what comprises curriculum content, as we have already demonstrated, wide and quite legitimate use is also made of principles other than those of didactics (philosophical, those drawn from the science of the subject itself, psychological, etc.). The contribution of non-didactic vis-à-vis didactic principles and their transformation into a system is a challenging and, in our opinion, basic problem requiring a solution.

This merits further comment. In applying the term 'norm' in the context of didactic principles, we are taking into account the widely varying notions covered. A norm is not necessarily an imperative, the more so as it is 'the use made of a sentence and not its "outward appearance" that makes it the formulation of a norm'[2].

Didactic principles serve to substantiate the method of applying the general principles of curriculum construction (see Section 3, Chapter I). Of these principles priority should be given to the *didactic characteristics of teaching.*

Among these characteristics, in turn, priority should be given to the *unity of the content- and process-related aspects of instruction.* This unity is classified with the above general principles because — as we have already said — it determines the role of practice in constructing and analysing curriculum content.

Another important characteristic of instruction is the *unity of teaching and learning.* This means that it is incumbent upon the teacher to identify the specific content to be learned in class. In actual teaching conditions, specific content may be expressed by the teacher in forms which vary according to, for example, the pupils' background, the amount of study time allotted for that subject, the need for additional teaching materials and, last but not least, with the teacher's individual character and approach. A creative teacher will never blindly follow the content handed down to him 'ready-made', since educational reality is just as unpredictable as any other form of reality.

This didactic principle derives from the previous one. Indeed, the teacher — or anyone who compiles material for the teacher — keeps the above factors in mind while constructing or improving content, since they are process-related.

Likewise deriving from a systems approach to the development of curriculum content and from the general principles underlying it is another didactic principle to be defined as *the necessity to take account of the functions of curriculum content in general and subject content in particular, as well as to bring the scope and structure of the study material into line with the functions that a particular subject performs within general education.*

The methods of applying this principle derive from its definition at the level of the school subject (see Section 4, Chapter I). Accordingly it is proposed to base the classification of these subjects on the role of each one in attaining the goals of general education[3].

Also deriving from this function are the main elements within each subject. Thus, the main element of subjects like physics, chemistry, biology, geography, history and astronomy is scientific knowledge, whereas the main element of subjects like foreign languages, draftsmanship, physical culture, as well as technology-related subjects, will be modes of activity (skills and useful habits). In teaching fine arts and music the goal is to mould in the pupils a particular vision of reality.

This classification is obviously more 'educationally biased' than that which is based on the given school subject representing a science and through it the group of sciences to which it belongs. The classification we are proposing here is derived from the goals of general education and the contribution of each subject to satisfying these goals. Accordingly, physics and history are classed under the same heading because of their role as school subjects and not as related sciences.

The clear identification of the classifying element is helpful towards rationalizing the structure of subject content, i.e. towards determining the quantitative and qualitative ratio of its various components. This is not to abolish the classification of school subjects on the alternative principle. The two classifications serve different purposes in contributing to curriculum content.

Putting this didactic principle into action may take the form of a scientific rationale, i.e. grouping school subjects according to a common function. Groups of school subjects can be identified according to common problems the solution of which is associated with a specific branch of scientific knowledge. This latter principle has been proposed for a group of science-related subjects so as to reduce their content to a comparatively small number of problems which sum up all the various aspects of the given area of knowledge[4]. Since the content of scientific subjects reflects the content and structure of the related sciences, the problems of these sciences are reflected in these science-related subjects. Therefore all common problems in a science serve as a basis upon which to construct a school subject on that science.

The experience so far gained in the countries with advanced education systems shows that devising adequate criteria for the selection of teaching material is a problem still defying solution. Prior to tackling it, one has to solve a number of theoretical problems, which, *inter alia*, involve answering two questions:

1. *What minimum curriculum content is to be acquired upon finishing secondary school?* In other words, what minimum knowledge is one supposed to acquire to be able to participate in a modern socialist society and to be able to keep pace with the march of progress? This question needs clarifying. The school simply cannot leave the young person to his own devices once he has graduated. A schoolchild does not stop being a child and in primary school one should not so much be concerned with getting him ready to live the life of a responsible citizen as with the special interests appropriate to his age. It is incumbent upon the educationist to set not only that minimum of content which is obligatory upon final graduation, but also that which is obligatory upon finishing primary and incomplete secondary school. As far as the Soviet school is concerned, it involves establishing the minimum content on completing four years, nine years and eleven years of study.

2. *What kind of curriculum is the optimum one to serve the educational goals of a typical Soviet school and what subjects and activities should it contain?* The latter question can be answered by defining 'subject' and subsequently 'study material'. But first, one has to locate the source to be used as a guide in constructing the content of general education, and the prime factors influencing this construction in the context of the Soviet school. It is in clarifying these questions that one provides grounds for awareness of the educational factors, an awareness which it is incumbent upon educationists to bring home to every teacher and instructor. Indeed, for all the objective character of factors to determine its composition, curriculum content is after all only an artificial arrangement made to the design of a group of educationists and other theorists. Resort to common sense and experience is not likely to furnish indisputable answers to these questions and may lead to erroneous conclusions. It is educational theory combined with experience and common sense that awakens in educationists and teachers alike a true awareness of the educational factors that are really adequate to solve the problems in hand.

Following the exhaustive discussion in Chapter II, our attention is now focused on more precise details of curriculum content. Social experience being a universal source of curriculum content, we still have to locate the more practical sources of that content as well as the factors affecting the actual use. A source of curriculum content is something that will yield precise subject-related material to be imparted to the younger generation. Although not comprising content, one factor does affect its construction — the selection process itself. Strictly speaking, since a source of content may also be a factor in its construction, one is free to define a factor in somewhat broader terms, perceiving two groups: that from which curriculum content is directly or indirectly drawn and that which affects its composition without yielding content material.

The dominant source, as we have already seen, is *social experience*. Its analysis has already led us to some useful conclusions concerning the four-element composition of curriculum content as a whole, as well as for each school subject, teaching material and the lesson in hand. This seemed to favour the assumption that, in compiling the minimum content for acquisition during primary, incomplete-secondary and complete secondary schools, the curriculum should contain all four elements of social experience.

Social experience can be analysed into *types of activity*. There are numerous such classifications available in the literature. We adhere to the following classification of disciplines: transforming reality, cognitive, communicative, evaluative and artistic[9]. These cover all the usual activities of people. This classification assumes that disciplines which correspond to all the five types of activity will be included into the content of general education. Since the elements of social experience (knowledge, modes of activity, creative experience and emotional attitudes) cannot exist other than in subject content or an activity, these five activity types, being a conceptualized image of reality, also exist in a branch of social activities. Therefore, the next source for establishing curriculum content is *the various spheres of reality*. As we have already said (see Chapter II), activities were the earliest source of curriculum content. They now have to be taken into consideration. It is branches of activity that determine the composition of curriculum, the total set of school subjects. Up to now, this problem has baffled attempts at solution. As the corresponding sciences and specializations widen in scope, new subjects are proposed for inclusion into curriculum, such as information science, elementary technology, civic education; subjects, such as the fundamentals of family relations as well as ethics and aesthetics have already been introduced on a trial basis. However,the value of such subjects remains to be seen, not to mention the proper use of time and the possibility of overburdening the pupil.

Thus, all these three sources (social experience, types of activity, specializations) have to be considered in order of priority in constructing curricula. Yet, we have so far little or no awareness of the educational factors. To enable a more adequate expression of the educational factor in content construction, one should bear in mind that each of the specializations selected for inclusion into the appropriate subject has to be adapted educationally, i.e. from the viewpoint of its necessity for general education, of its being understandable by the pupil, and that it occupies a logical position in a consecutive order of space and time. Indeed, neither type of activity nor specialization can be acquired without resorting to some sort of auxiliary material. Based on the logic of the gradual revelation of a subject, auxiliary material is selected to be included in content. This material must of necessity be composed of brief items, yet, one cannot dispense with it. Typically, all textbook authors and all teachers are constantly searching for ways to render study materials available; but not to the detriment of brevity.

The conditions determining the acquisition of the elements of content may also serve as a source. The learning process is impossible without various types of perception and memorizing activity; comprehension through association, imagination, problem-oriented situations, transferring knowledge to new situations, physical activities, comparative activities, confirming one's own solution, resorting to different types of reasoning, etc. All these activities are fit for inclusion into curriculum content and are helpful in acquiring subject-related content. But to make instruction really work they should be integrated into a system. Usually, this aspect is left out of the curriculum, but in the process of learning it inevitably plays a role. Yet, if curriculum compilers are not properly aware of its role and do not think it fit for inclusion, this is bound to reduce the effectiveness of teaching.

Teaching methods are still another source of content. Since teaching methods suggest teacher/pupil interaction, the pupil also needs to have some idea of the elements of teaching activity, such as verbal presentation, the communicative techniques of various teachers, the use of rhetorical questions, techniques of designing and posing questions, techniques to explain objects and processes, as well as of organizing one's own learning activity. Since teaching methods are realized through teaching techniques, these latter being employed by teachers in large numbers, each new teaching technique is not only a means of instruction, but also part of curriculum content.

Study materials are another constantly growing and just as constantly changing source of content. Additional content to be acquired may also involve punched cards, partly printed workbooks, calculating machines, etc.

Standing somewhat apart as a source of content are local influences which may complement and transform core curricula, such as the natural, demographic, national, household, social, psychological and cultural situation.

And finally, the teacher's personality, personal style, techniques, approach to his class, and the changes he introduces in the lesson also comprise a source of curriculum content, even though of a different nature. Of course, the contribution from this source varies with the teacher's personality. However, it is always compatible with and subordinate to the established core curriculum.

All these sources are linked in a definite manner, some of them hierarchically, others on equal terms, but as far as content construction goes, they are not interchangeable and each has to be reckoned with as an individual item.

So far we have inventoried the elements comprising curriculum content as well as the analytically identifiable models of the teaching process[10]. However, one should devote attention to the boundaries between them. They indicate the likely areas where curriculum content is to be found and this is most clear as far as social experience is concerned. Yet, this is not sufficient for the selection of content appropriate to each branch of activity. For that one needs more precise criteria. Exception must be made for such sources as acquisition practices, the methods, means and organization of teaching and sources yielding reliable content.

There are, as we have already said, factors which, without being sources of content, do affect the approach to or selection of content. The factor of primary importance affecting the construction of curriculum content is the goals put before education by society. Thus, society may set the relatively narrow goal of socialization of the younger generation. Or else, it may strive for the goal of moulding socially-involved, broad-minded people with a profound humanitarian attitude. In both cases, social demands, even though not comprising curriculum content, do determine the content selected from various sources, such as different kinds of knowledge and skills, stress on knowledge of theory as against practical activities, greater or smaller differentiation of various specializations for different groups of pupils, etc.

Another factor affecting the scope of content and the way of imparting it is the learning capacity of the overwhelming majority of pupils. Recognizing the need to grant all young people a uniform general education, the Soviet school system lays stress on content that is understandable to all pupils, that avoids overburdening the pupils with non-essentials, but maintains the high standards of education. With this in mind, any planned variation in content is subject to evaluation for its understandability by pupils.

This is designed to ensure that the general education system is suitable for all. At the same time, it is strongly advisable to take into account that pupils have different inclinations and abilities in various specializations, such as mathematics, music, technology, drawing, physics, history, typing, embroidery, crafts, etc. The pupils performing best in a particular field should be given the opportunity of acquiring a content going beyond the limits of the general content. For such pupils resort should be made to out-of-school opportunities (optional courses, special interest groups, etc.).

Striking a balance between these two factors enables the general culture of the younger generation to be raised and the individual requirements of every individual pupil to be satisfied. The more able pupils will benefit by differentiated pre-vocational training which will encourage the pupil to develop personal abilities by going deeper into a chosen field and acquiring appropriate skills.

All the above factors to a varying degree are common to any society planning the

84The theory of curriculum content in the USSR

content of education. The factors can be rationally and exhaustively understood only when curriculum designers reach a certain level of awareness of educational factors. Thus, already for some time past in many countries the characteristics of learning have been studied in a haphazard manner. It appears incumbent upon educationists to define precise criteria for the selection of basic content common to all subjects, a content which would be affected by such factors as teaching methods and materials, ways of organizing classes and the characteristics of learning.

Although they are common to many school systems, all these factors are inevitably subject to different approaches depending on the nature of society, the criteria that society applies to the education and socialization of the young, the goals that society expects of education, the specific demands of a society which dictate the principles underlying curriculum construction.

The following principles would seem to determine the compilation of curricula, textbooks and teaching in the USSR.

(a) curriculum content based on contemporary progress in science and technology;
(b) a view of the world which is based on conformity with a materialist worldview at the level of science and theory;
(c) a humanitarian orientation of curriculum content in harmony with the social, moral and aesthetic ideals of Soviet society;
(d) curriculum content which has been compiled in a spirit of optimism and faith in greater social justice for all;
(e) curriculum content which will contribute to a socially active, creative personality ready to undertake any kind of work;
(f) inculcation of love of the motherland and a respect for all nations and cultures;
(g) maintaining a firm link with life and its everyday problems by specifying that curricula should apply knowledge and active methods which stress their practical importance;
(h) maintaining the pupils' physical development at a high standard.

These principles — for all their clarity — still need further refinement. For the present, we limit our detailed discussion on one of these points, partly to illustrate the ways these principles are formulated and partly to elucidate their role. This is the principle of curriculum construction in conformity with Soviet society's worldview.

Throughout history, there has invariably been a certain worldview and, in the modern society, there has even been a philosophy behind formal education or any deliberate form of education whenever it has been reflected in curriculua and textbooks. The designers of curriculum content have not always been aware of the existence of this worldview, but it has influenced education. At present, there are no two opinions on that subject among educationists. In constructing curriculum content, Soviet theorists draw upon *dialectical materialism*, not merely to give them an impartial perspective, but indeed as a tool at every stage of this construction. Both in curricula and textbooks, as well as in teaching as such, it has four functions to perform: as a goal of education; as a guide in constructing its content; as a means of designing this content; and, last but not least, as part of this content. This worldview has to perform the function of a goal as long as the school seeks to make it a personal value with every pupil. It acts as a guide in that it influences concepts which form attitudes and are expressed in implicit, empirical form, especially in the early years of teaching. Next, it serves as a means to construct curriculum content, a yardstick to determine the raw material needed to express in educational terms the various aspects of the system of ideas and principles. And finally, the basic ideas and principles comprising dialectical materialism form part of the lesson. This content should be inculcated in the pupils to become their spiritual credo and a fundamental component in their personal system of values.

Thus, a worldview serves as a source to draw upon in designing the actual content of education, as well as a principle to underlie its construction.

The proper forum to debate attitudinal problems is the literature of philosophy. This is, however, not to deny the right of the educational sciences to contribute to this issue. What is essential to that science is to identify the stages in the formation of attitudes, the criteria to judge whether attitudes have or have not been formed, the functions of different types and different depths of knowledge on the development of attitudes, and, finally, the order of priority of attitude components in constructing curriculum content.

A world outlook may be utilitarian or academic. The former is common, even among the semi-literate. An academic attitude is typical of an individual capable of giving a theoretical explanation of his view of the world and his behaviour, and this involves a philosophical background. The Soviet school is concerned with broadening the pupils' outlook, and lays emphasis on a view of the world based on a scientifically substantiated system of philosophical and socio-political concepts. This goal is attainable only by including philosophical and associated knowledge into curriculum content. Yet, philosophy alone is not enough. It is also essential that each generation should be familiar with the way scientific and sociological views of the world have developed throughout history. The sociological background of life assumes knowledge of the laws, principles and prospects that govern the development of modern human society. Society needs socially active members capable of creatively transforming that society along progressive and humanistic lines.

To understand how one's attitude and attitude-forming knowledge are to be reflected in curricula, and particularly in textbooks, one should bear in mind that one's attitude is an *alter ego* expressing itself in one's social behaviour and not reducible to knowledge of reality. It serves as a guide to activity and the individual is usually aware of this orienting function. Attitude has a dual structure. Thus, the idea of progress as part of attitude is embodied in the mind not only as the idea of social development being progressive but also as the idea that one should actually contribute to that progress. Another example. The idea of social upheaval as an important factor of existence in a socially stratified society is hardly new. This concept will not influence attitudes until its acquirer understands the need to view social phenomena in terms of contradictions.

We do not seek to survey all factors which influence attitudes in curricula. However, we are trying to emphasize that each factor and principle we have inventoried so far should be examined individually in order to identify its particular role.

Types of activity and specializations in curriculum content. As we have already said in Chapter II, knowledge of the composition of social experience is not enough to construct a model of curriculum content. This composition has first to be subdivided into types of activity and specializations. The five types of activity which have already been inventoried have to be further subdivided into, as it were, building blocks to account for even the tiniest unit in curriculum content. These small details may prove vital in getting every member of the younger generation ready to perform the multiple functions required by society. Šubinski has made a study of this subdivision. He analyses activity types into practical, social and spiritual, each of which is still further broken down as follows:

Practical activities include: self-help; help to others; work in school workshops and gardens; in-service training; staging experiments in the school laboratory; making footpaths; nature conservation; improving facilities in school and, if possible, out of school.

Social activities include: participation in social events, dissemination of culture; helping the younger children organize themselves; maintaining discipline in the school and its environs; presenting reports on topical issues; self-management participation in school; practising leadership at the school level; practising communication at the inter-personal and group levels; learning to organize leisure time; everyday family life (home economics, hygiene and family education); helping poor achievers; self-education and self-socialization; learning self-hygiene and practising physical culture.

Cultural activities include: knowing how to learn in class and out of class; gaining experience establishing one's own set of values; and developing one's positive emotions and feelings (appreciating moral and aesthetic values, learning to share feelings with others, to express one's emotions and attitudes).

This list is an indication in itself that curriculum content can and should include activities reserved not only for the classroom but also those that take place far beyond its walls. It is important, however, that these activities are designed and programmed in the school. Only then will they form part of the system of curriculum content.

It is obvious that the elements of social experience form part of any activity and hence of any combination of activities, of any specialization. In other words, no single type of activity includes all specializations, even though each specialization may include more than one type or several types of activity. Thus, a productive or cultural (painting, music) activity may also involve organizational, communicative and self-evaluative sub-activities. And yet activity types are not interchangeable, even though each of them contains all the four elements of social experience. Hence, one can teach creativity and sensitivity within a narrow range of activities, but this range of activities is too restricted to be used for a broadly educated personality. In this case, there is a need to involve a person into all types of activity which are to be embodied into the specializations selected for general education.

Whatever the degree of education for whatever group of young people, an initial impetus will always be the need for society to reproduce the conditions of its existence and hence its productive capacity, however diverse the demand for manpower may be. It therefore follows that attention should focus on production as a major influence on curriculum content.

In the early history of mankind, preparing young people for productive activity would have been limited to handicrafts, i.e. training that did not require general education. The artisan would not learn the principles underlying his actions or the laws governing technology in his chosen field. Be it smelting, weaving, glass-blowing or tool-making, it was enough for the tradesman engaged in these activities to have a thorough grasp of the standardized procedures and to gain practical experience. In centuries past illiterate and semi-literate workers performed their jobs perfectly well within the requirements of technology and productivity.

In the modern period of technical and scientific progress, production can no longer be maintained by workers whose education is limited to their particular trade. The demand for broadly educated workers is constantly increasing and so are their qualifications. With the advent of large-scale mechanization and automation, the machine has removed the burden of production off man's shoulders. With an increase in the complexity of machines there is a corresponding transfer of man-power to their servicing, maintenance and repair[11]. Maintenance technicians, the number of whom increases accordingly, have to have some knowledge of automation, precision engineering, electronics, hydraulic engineering and mechanics. These and other branches of knowledge have to be mastered by the worker in view of the rapid and constant changes in technology within the lapse of a single generation. Workers must both adapt to this change and extend their knowledge to new fields. Without an adequate educational background such an adaptation is hardly feasible. Furthermore, the worker is no longer confined to performing one function; the number of operations he has to perform is constantly increasing.

The Soviet worker has long ceased to be a mere agent of the will of others. Increasingly, he tends to understand his own role in production and, indeed, is asked to participate in decision making on economic and organizational problems, as well as suggesting improvements in the social field. This participative approach assumes that the worker is conversant with economics, management, social psychology, ethics, etc. Soviet industry needs innovative workers. They should not only have the necessary knowledge and skills but, indeed, be prepared to improve production on their own initiative and in as creative a manner as possible. There is a rapid increase in the number of innovators among the workers who often co-operate with designers and engineers in search of new solutions. Indeed, modern production requires a worker who has had some schooling in scientific reasoning and is not altogether foreign to the logic of learning.

In this perspective, the school is called upon to impart broadly based knowledge both in the natural sciences and the humanities so that on finishing school young men and women are ready to master virtually any industrial trade or office job. Providing training of this kind would seem to favour polytechnical education, a form of education which would end the outdated divisions between specializations and move towards greater integration on a broad technical and scientific basis. Polytechnical education makes young people familiar with those skills which are common to all branches of activity, and with machines and processes typically found in several industries. Young people acquire the rudiments of as many trades as possible. This function of polytechnical training grows in importance with the integration of various industries on a common technical and scientific foundation, and it is incumbent upon modern formal education to contribute to this dynamic process.

Naturally, the scientific level of general education has to keep pace with progress.

But social demands on general education do not end there. Raising the quality of general education is one of the purposes of Soviet society. Therefore one of the objectives of the educational sciences aims at the all-round development of the personality and the formation of socially active citizens who possess a scientific approach, whose intellectual powers are highly developed and who have a creative capacity. It is time to determine the limits in general education which would adequately reflect the progress of modern science.

We have already touched upon the principle of the use of scientific methods in establishing curriculum content, a principle that has always guided the Soviet school. Today, it is examined in three dimensions: 1. curriculum content should reflect modern scientific progress; 2. this content should give pupils some idea of methods prevalent in a particular science and common to all sciences; 3. it should make the basic laws of learning understandable to the pupils[12].

Keeping pace with progress assumes that curriculum content has nothing in it that is foreign to modern science, that falsifies current scientific concepts. Both the natural sciences and humanities studied in school should be thoroughly purged of unscientific notions. Besides, the pupils have to have a general idea about science itself if they are to acquire a logical style of reasoning. They should learn to reflect upon everyday happenings in their true setting, as well as upon the very process of learning about reality. Science should be presented to the pupils as a logical system of knowledge undergoing constant development, and this also applies to the process of learning itself which is governed by precise norms and practices.

A science may be regarded as a system of concepts and as a system of theories, depending on the level of its development. But irrespective of this, a science can be divided into subject-related knowledge, knowledge of specific learning methods and knowledge of its own history. Scientific knowledge is embodied in concepts, facts, laws, theories, hypotheses, problems and a scientific view of reality. In the school subjects reflecting the essentials of sciences (physics, chemistry, biology, astronomy, history, geography), the basic theories of these sciences find their educational expression. Thus, the course of physics is supposed to contain the essentials of five theories: that of macrobodies in mechanical motion; that of thermodynamics; molecular-kinetic theory; the theory of electro-dynamics; and the theory of relativity (which stands somewhat apart). The school course of chemistry essentially consists of Mendeleev's theories of inorganic chemistry and the theories of organic structure.

The study of sciences in school is supposed to furnish such basic skills as observation and handling laboratory equipment, using tables, maps, graphs, handbooks, etc. Furthermore, science is expected to mould an evaluative attitude toward reality including the truth and the process of discovering it. Science embodied in school subjects stimulates diligence, objective reasoning, self-criticism and responsibility.

The content of science courses at school varies with the age and intellectual capacity of pupils. In presenting a theory in class it is very important to follow its structure consistently[13].

Science being not only a system of knowledge but also an activity, the pupils should be introduced to the logic and stages of scientific learning, methods and learning practices. The methods of learning and presentation are inevitable components of the content of those school subjects which correspond to sciences. Learning methods may be empirical or theoretical. Curriculum content is supposed to include, *inter alia*, those more particular methods which are of significance in general education.

The history of science is particularly valuable for the pupils in that it demonstrates the activity of scientists and the value of scientific discoveries for the people in general.

The subjects in the curriculum also have to reflect such trends in modern science as integration and synthesis. Also deserving mention is a trend for modern scientific theories to cover an ever greater field of knowledge with every passing year. This trend has already led to a greater stress on theoretical knowledge. Curriculum content is also affected by the increasing role of mathematics in science and the decreasing role of visualization in mechanical terms. Modern trends also give a greater role to the use of science as a productive force. These trends are embodied in curriculum content to encourage a scientific style of reasoning and a capacity for self-reflection.

3. DIDACTIC BASES FOR COMPILING CURRICULUM CONTENT

Syllabus and subject. Up to now we have concerned ourselves with a general idea of the composition of curriculum content and, briefly, with the role of some of its sources. Yet, in order that curriculum content as a whole should serve all-round development of the personality, its elements must have substance. But first one has to imagine what a well-developed personality is like and, if this goal has not been achieved, what elements need to be acquired.

In other words, what one has to imagine is that ideal minimum of content which is to be acquired by every pupil (or an overwhelming majority of pupils) on completing general education, whatever their individual aptitudes might be. This is one of the problems that bedevil education and that defy any properly substantiated solution, a problem that has hitherto been subject to empirical and pragmatic solutions. Neither can the authors of the present discourse propose a fully adequate solution. For the time being we will limit our discussion to a few approaches to the solution of this problem which have been derived from the theory and practice of Soviet education.

We have arrived at the conclusion that curriculum content comprises four elements of social experience and five types of activity. Now we set out to identify those specializations which are supposed to express the entire content. But curriculum content consists not only of school subjects studied in the classroom but also of that part of content which is acquired out of class during organized social activity, games and other forms of leisure. It is also an objective to train pupils to participate in different social activities such as family life, profitable use of leisure time, etc.

Identifying the principal fields of activity will take another step forward if the identifier comes to realize the need to give the pupils physical, mental, work-oriented, communicative, moral, aesthetic, ideological and cultural education, i.e. elements which set a general pattern for personality development to follow. Once this need has been appreciated, it becomes easier to identify the essential branches of human activity. The significance of physical education is obvious enough. It stimulates physical development through exercises virtually from the cradle, inculcating an appetite for sport and encouraging the pupils to take constant exercise during their school years and after. Next, the pupils should acquire such vital abilities as proper speech habits, writing and calculating skills, and logical reasoning, which are prerequisites to any further activity. Manual training is the next item on the list of skills which are supposed to maintain human society since it leads to productive work in industrial enterprises. It is in school that one should learn to work in a variety of ways. The future worker should know how to help himself and others, should be familiar with the school workshop and should be given an opportunity to participate in on-the-job training. On-the-job training means that the pupils work at special enterprises associated with the school which provide out-of-school manual training using up-to-date equipment or even at real factories and plants with the aid of educationally-experienced supervisors. Since production trends vary from region to region, on-the-job training of pupils is not so much aimed at mastering a particular trade (such as operating a loom or a lathe) as at acquiring the general knowledge, skills and techniques characteristic of production as a whole. In this way, the pupil is expected not only to upgrade his general education but also to gain the necessary background which will permit him to master any productive job shortly after leaving school.

At the same time, to facilitate work-oriented training or any other process leading to successful performance in most present-day activities, one should not neglect the pupils' intellectual development. Intellectual development in the form of acquiring sound knowledge, methods of reasoning and learning have by now become a major goal of teaching. Yet, there remains the question of which sciences in particular one should select for inclusion in formal education. Debate on this problem is now underway practically the world over and it is no accident that the inventory of such subjects differs from country to country reflecting different interests. In the USSR it is also proposed now and then to introduce into the curriculum such subjects as the rudiments of technology, ethics, etc.[14]. Apart from the burden on curriculum and the limits on study time, one still has to convince curriculum compilers of the validity of these new subjects.

Supposedly helpful in selecting sciences for inclusion into school curricula as subjects is their classification by object of study (minerals; organisms; society; man; reasoning), and their further classification into particular fields of knowledge (natural sciences, technical sciences, mathematics, humanities). Yet, these classifications are no more than a guide to indicate the likely areas in which to look for suitable sciences for school subjects. It stands to reason that the most suitable are fundamental disciplines which serve as a basis for other sciences. Such fundamental disciplines are philosophy, mathematics, cybernetics, physics, geophysics, chemistry, biology, history, and the technical sciences complemented by such auxiliary practical skills as draftsmanship, etc.[15].

All the above considerations are still inadequate for selecting the optimum number and configuration of subjects for study. For instance, the obvious need for communication training necessitates the study of the mother tongue and foreign languages. The study of aesthetic appreciation also implies greater stress on literature and on innovative methods to introduce children to music, such as those proposed by the outstanding Soviet composer Kabalevskij, as well as on the study of drawing and clay modelling. In some countries, there is a course of ethics in school which serves the purpose of moral socialization. In the USSR, the study of ethics is a non-obligatory subject. We believe that moral training should form part of all subjects, the more so as the content of each subject in the Soviet school invariably includes some elements of a humanistic nature and there is some part of the teaching process where such an attitude is imparted.

The inventory of specializations does not end there. There are also those outside the limits of subjects and teaching. The pupils must also learn to conduct themselves in the social field, to use their leisure time usefully, to play games and to be a good partner in the family — in the economic, educational and communicative senses. All these activities are of special importance in guiding intellectual and moral aspects of personality development, and in building up a system of personal values. One criterion that has lately been gaining ground in international literature on education, which suggests that the rationality of an individual's life style can be judged by the manner in which he spends his leisure time, is suitable for adoption, in our view, as a very precise yardstick. Yet, this criterion still needs improvement both as far as outward indications go and the means to identify aspects of leisure behaviour that elucidate the need for cultural pursuits and humanistic attitudes.

Such are in general outline certain ideas which may lead to the construction of a properly justified minimum content of general secondary education. They are, and this should be emphasized, only tentative ideas and, to become true guidelines for initiating compilation, they have to be further elaborated, codified and refined.

It is fair to conclude that, in the first place, the curriculum should incorporate not only school subjects and the time limits governing the teaching of these subjects, but also out-of-class and out-of-school activities which are conducive to all-round development. Just as their subject counterparts taught in class, these activities should cover productive work, social pursuits and physical training, and should express humanistic attitudes to be inculcated in the pupils.

In the second place, in constructing a subject curriculum it is necessary to identify and justify the minimum content of general education for the four-year elementary school, nine-year incomplete secondary and eleven-year secondary school which are successive steps towards universal, compulsory, complete secondary education. An obligatory minimum should be laid down for each subject, irrespective of specialization, in order to avoid the danger of splitting knowledge into isolated subjects.

So far we have been discussing school subjects as something self-evident. Yet, the concept of a school subject needs individual attention, since it is at the level of consolidating content that subjects are resolved into a detailed design. One of the major deficiencies of modern education originates, in our view, from a lack of a clear understanding of the educational character and composition of school subjects.

For some time past a school subject has been looked upon either as a reflection of the corresponding science (physics, history, biology, etc.), or as a reflection of the content of an activity (physical culture, languages, draftsmanship, handicrafts, etc.). Such an interpretation has long been felt to be erroneous among educationists. In

1969, this matter came under discussion in the USSR[16]. The greater clarity which resulted, however, has been slow to alter the established thinking on the subject on the part of curriculum and textbook compilers. This is at least partly explained by the absence of an adequate psychologically-backed answer to a number of difficulties and the consequent lack of substantiation of certain points raised in the discussion.

Today, we are witnessing a renewal of interest in this problem in view of recent advances in a number of concepts concerning the general theory of curriculum content.

'School subject' may be tentatively defined as part of content which is unfolded over a period of time in a content-related and educational sequence and which is acquired through instruction. The content of a school subject thus comprises activity in a given field, such as, if we take chemistry for example, skills pertaining to chemistry and also the activity of acquiring skills. It follows that a school subject should consist of:

— content reflecting social experience in a particular field;
— the basic elements of a particular vocation as taught in general education;
— the content associated with presenting the basic elements of a particular vocation and with the methods of acquiring them;
— content associated with the methods of teaching;
— content associated with communicative activity in the process of teaching.

Thus, a school subject is an educational phenomenon combining in itself the content of subject-related and teaching-related activities. If one does not accept this breakdown of a school subject there is a danger of neglecting the role the educational sciences should play in teaching. Teaching based on intuition, common sense and tradition is obviously inadequate to achieve a satisfactory level of results. The instruction of a particular school subject depends not only on the schoolteacher but also on its relationship with other subjects. A school subject is made up of two blocks: content-related and process-related. The latter enables the acquisition of the former; it is the means of acquisition. The composition of both blocks depends on the particular school subject. The functions of school subjects derive not only from content but also from the purpose they serve in the curriculum. The traditional division of subjects into streams — natural sciences and humanities — is not sufficient in this case. Since the functions of school subjects are associated with the dominant component of their content, that component may serve as a basis for their classification into:

1. Subjects with knowledge as a dominant component (physics, chemistry, biology, geography, history, astronomy);
2. Subjects with modes of activity (skills) as a dominant component (foreign languages, draftsmanship, physical culture, technical disciplines, manual training);
3. Subjects with an evaluative and emotional interpretion of reality as a dominant component (drawing, music).

There are subjects with two dominant components: mother tongue, mathematics (knowledge and skills); poetry and literature (knowledge and emotional attitudes).

In each of the above three groups the two blocks (content-related and process-related — which functions as an auxiliary) differ in content. The concept of a school subject[17] goes a long way towards clarifying the issue which up to now has been a major point of controversy. According to some authors, instruction by subjects stands in the way of integrated knowledge. In our view, it is the difference between types of subjects that makes the construction of an adequate integrated curriculum impossible. Furthermore, the existence of discrete school subjects reflects the continuing differentiation between sciences. It is possible to achieve the integration of knowledge in school by introducing such broad subjects as natural history, general biology and social sciences in junior forms and by establishing connections between subjects during or towards the conclusive stages of study. The next step may be to explore the possibility of constructing a discipline that unifies all the natural science subjects.

The school subject embodied in the curriculum and textbooks needs principles and criteria in order to select its content.

Principles and criteria for selecting curriculum content. The problem of curriculum construction, which assumes decisions on the selection of knowledge, is a matter of concern for educationists everywhere. School subjects are constructed on the basis of tradition, empiricism, reliance on non-educational expertise, in short, on the subjective opinions of curriculum compilers. There are countries in which each school has its own nomenclature of subjects and their assembly into curricula is left entirely to the compilers' discretion. The educational sciences have not yet come up with a truly scientific substantiation of the ways and means of constructing school subjects, neither have they devised a curriculum theory consisting of definite premises based on well-founded conclusions that could serve as a yardstick upon which to select the content of school subjects.

The purpose of this book is to sum up the results of attempts at constructing precisely such a theory and identifying in it normative guidelines which could contribute to compiling the content of school subjects.

We have presented a number of points to be taken into consideration when compiling curricula. We have also dwelt on the definition of a 'school subject', the construction of which is the principal goal of the theory of educational content. The compilation of each particular subject is undertaken by methodologists compiling curricula and textbooks. At the same time, since there are certain common elements between all school subjects and between some of their groups, it is incumbent on a didactic theory of curriculum content to identify general guidelines for the compilation of individual subjects or groups of subjects. These guidelines are didactic rationales and criteria for content selection. These rationales indicate the general direction along which to select content, while the criteria determine particular items of content along this general direction.

Didactic guidelines follow a somewhat hierarchical pattern, some of them being of a more general character, others of a more specific character and subordinate to the former. The more general principles for the construction of a school subject include the goal of teaching, the elements of social experience, types of activity and specializations from which other branches of activity derive. All these principles have already been examined earlier in this book.

Another example of a general didactic guideline is the idea that for the content of formal education one should select all that is of general educational value, i.e. content which plays an important role in all spheres of human activity carried out by all the members of a given society, or at least that which should play such a role in the future. This kind of content may have two forms: (a) applicable to a particular subject, such as that of writing, reading, arithmetic, knowledge of human anatomy, basic chemistry, national and world history, information science; (b) universally applicable, i.e. a form suitable for any particular content, such as logical thinking, research skills, creativity, managerial skills, constructive use of time, leisure, etc.

All these guidelines cannot be regarded as adequate even at the level of didactics, since they do no more than indicate the general direction along which to select content and the broad spheres of reality from which content is to be extracted. A truly didactic theory of curriculum content should provide more precise guidelines for content selection.

Now for the selection of knowledge. For those science subjects where knowledge is integrated into exhaustive theories, a theory is a unit of content[18]. Therefore, all the fundamental theories — of which in physics there are five and in chemistry and biology two respectively — are to be included in the above subjects. Each of the theories should comprise basic concepts, basic laws and a minimum of conclusions. This set of different pieces of knowledge makes an integral theory, while a set of fundamental theories should give a truly scientific image of reality. In clarifying these criteria it is fair to point out that the number of concepts depends on the formulation of basic laws. The number of laws on the rudiments of a theory to be included into a school subject should equal that of the basic laws in the theory itself. The conclusions should derive from basic premises, yet their number should be reduced to a minimum. Any supplementary information should only be included if it substantiates the basic concept or demonstrates its functions. Additional knowledge not integrated into theories should only be included if it is of practical application, useful in imparting certain attitudes and polytechnical in character. Non-theoretical knowledge is subordinate to knowledge included in theories.

The history of science has a significant role to play in the matrix of natural science subjects. The principles for selecting this background knowledge include its role: in influencing attitudes and in motivating learning; in demonstrating our understanding of reality; in elucidating the learning process (controversies, crises and their resolution); in demonstrating the evolution of ideas and the historical evolution of knowledge; and in revealing the dependence of scientific progress on the development of production.

The share of the history of science in subject content will be determined by its importance in developing a scientific style of reasoning, in familiarizing the pupils with intricate experiments and in demonstrating the role of false concepts and paradoxes in the history of science. And finally, it should be stressed that historical material, for all the limitations on study time, should be presented as a vivid pageant of ideas, as a sequence of conflicts and victories, and as the contribution to science by one's own and other nations.

The selection of knowledge for formal education from the sciences should be guided by such didactic principles as the necessity to inculcate the idea of scientific knowledge being systematic, the necessity for knowledge to be unified into an integral theory, the necessity for auxiliary knowledge which contributes towards understanding the first two groups of knowledge, emphasis on revealing the attitude forming and polytechnical potential of knowledge, demonstrating the evolution of scientific knowledge, and emphasizing the social role of science, as well as its moral and aesthetic value[19].

Subjects not based on exhaustive theories (geography, law, literature, etc.), also have potential for forming attitudes, and providing polytechnical education and socialization within general education. Thus, the selection of facts from history will be determined by the way the teaching of a science is expected to influence the attitude of young people towards the past, by the possibilities of quoting historical facts to provoke a discussion on attitude formation, socio-political and moral problems, as well as citing historical facts that are likely to impress the pupils.

For those subjects which are concerned mainly with modes of activity, the selection of knowledge is determined by the necessity to provide guidelines. This applies to manual training, language study, draftsmanship and to the arts subjects.

An important didactic principle for the compilation of a school subject is the selection of the most succinct sequence to reveal the basic theories, laws and practices. The gradual unfolding of this sequence depends for success on additional content in the shape of information and examples. This additional material must be kept to a minimum, not, however, at the expense of comprehensibility.

Also suitable for inclusion into curriculum content are those perrenial socio-scientific problems (at a level comprehensible to the pupils) the solution of which may take a long time but which are very important to the progress of society as a whole.

And finally, it is necessary to envisage inter-subject connections in the matrix conducive to the integration of knowledge and the transference of active methods from system to system. Integration may help towards a better and broader understanding of reality.

So much for the didactic principles for selecting knowledge.

The didactic principles for selecting modes of activity (skills) differ from those for selecting knowledge, yet there are many 'shared' principles, such as their importance for general education, their potential in forming attitudes, their utility in manual training and in preparing the pupils to perform as citizens, etc. As for the selection of skills for curriculum content, these principles are too vague to be useful. There is a need for more facts.

One such principle is the set of skills to be included into curriculum content and mentioned earlier in this book. Yet, this is not enough, since it is necessary to identify principles for selecting skills within each type of activity. This task can be expedited by analysing learning in the matrix of instructional practice.

There are three groups of skills within learning activity. *The first group comprises subject-related methods*, such as those used to solve problems in mathematics and physics, design experiments, calculate historical dates, analyse literary characters, describe social movements, explain how to operate a lathe, carry out technical drawing, explain spelling and writing, use maps, tables and diagrams, etc.

For selecting skills under this heading one has to imagine the situations in which subject-related knowledge will be used and subsequently to identify the knowledge vital for general education, i.e. its contribution to other spheres of human activity and general culture from the practical, attitude forming, moral, social, aesthetic and other viewpoints. Subject-related knowledge may be divided into two sub-groups: (a) practical skills and procedures following precise rules (declension, conjugation, the four operations in arithmetic, perspective, etc.); (b) intellectual procedures which vary according to content including: explaining laws and experiments, and particular phenomena by referring to laws and theories; identifying the true objectives of a particular social system and the role its representatives play in the politics they pursue; determining the properties of a chemical substance by its composition, etc. There are vast numbers of such procedures for every school subject and we limit ourselves to these particular examples. It is possible now to surmize that all the knowledge comprising curriculum content is applied knowledge, an important fact in constructing that content. Yet, the ways to apply that knowledge may be very different indeed. In fact, there are four levels of its application.

The first level is that of identifying an object by its characteristics (the difference between a lake and a sea, the characteristics of a feudal manor, etc.).

The second level is that of implementing an unambiguous rule by strict step-by-step actions (the right-hand rule in physics, the traffic code, telling the right bank of a river from the left, taking one's bearings in the field and forest without a compass, etc.).

The third level is that of presenting material in a logical pattern with essential points being indicated by the teacher, but with the pupils having to subdivide these points into individual steps and then having to carry them out. Thus, in imparting methodological knowledge to the pupils, i.e. knowledge about knowledge and about learning, they are confronted with the following sequence in a scientific theory: (a) main purpose of the theory; (b) a particular purpose of the theory; (c) essentials of the theory (sources, concepts, premises, data); (d) instruments of the theory (mathematical and logical operations); (e) conclusions and their confirmation; (f) field of application[20]. These steps in the exposition of a theory enable the pupil to consolidate his knowledge of the theory; something he can only do by himself.

The fourth level is that of applying ideas which indicate the main direction of activity yet do not specify the method. This sort of knowledge is exemplified in any theory or idea. For example, a general philosophical concept might be that human thought or the culture of a particular period are, in the final analysis, determined by the contemporary conditions of existence. It is incumbent upon the pupil himself to identify the research method to find a particular explanation of the sources for a particular *cultural phenomenon*.

All four levels of knowledge application should be present in the compilation of curricula and textbooks. Thus, the first group of active methods — subject-related — depends upon the situations in which the curricular knowledge is applied, of the methods developed in the given sphere of activity and of the four levels of knowledge application.

The second group of active methods is common to all or at least many school subjects; without these methods one finds it hard to imagine any teaching activity at all. They are an essential prerequisite to applying the first-group methods. *Second-group methods are divided into sensory, motor and mental.* Among the mental methods of great importance are such habits as analysis, synthesis, comparison, classification, conceptualization, etc. Through frequent employment, these habits become automatic for the pupils, so they are soon able to transfer them into new situations, whether similar or dissimilar. This group heading also contains all the modes of activity leading to the acquisition of knowledge and skills, i.e. methods of perception, understanding what is perceived, of associating one item of knowledge with another, of gaining experience in the performance of operations, of revealing knowledge according to a known pattern, of varying methods, etc.

Also included under the second-group heading are searching skills. These skills means comparing the parameters of a problem with one another and with what is to be achieved, comparing operations in the course of solution with one another and comparing the final outcome with what was to be done, demonstrating the relevance and logic of every operation which contributes to a solution, and demonstrating and confirming the final solution.

Learning techniques are included under the third group of methods, i.e. methods to organize the activity of acquiring subject content. These methods, without being the means of acquisition, are actually implicated in its organization. Methods which are applicable to all subjects and suitable for inclusion into curriculum content include such commonly known techniques as: précis-writing, memorization, fluency in reading and writing, using reference books and cataloguing. Less familiar methods are also used, such as: planning and timing one's work, verifying a spoken or written statement and correcting it if necessary, using maps, graphs and tables, presenting one's ideas in visual form, performing operations with precision and neatness, taking notes in reading and précis-writing, presenting problems clearly, thinking out moves and decisions beforehand, reformulating one's ideas, presenting material in a logical sequence, reflecting upon the operations performed, etc.

*   *   *

So far we have discussed a number of didactic principles applicable to various school subjects which indicate the general directions along which one should proceed in constructing curriculum content. But it is also necessary to provide more detail on the compilation of curriculum guidelines which are applicable to all or at least many subjects. Even though we are unable to come up with criteria to select in every case optimum lesson material, as well as to reject what is non-essential, yet we believe it useful to outline criteria that would at least contribute something to the present situation, thereby making the content of school subjects more relevant.

Experiments have been conducted recently in search of methods to develop the pupils' creative potential[21, 22, 23]. Since they have yielded findings that may have bearing upon this discussion, we would like to say a few words about them. The researchers were seeking short cuts to developing the pupils' intellect through teaching them to find creative solutions to problem-oriented tasks included in curricular material. However, the whole field is vast and cannot be considered ideal for the purpose of problem-solving. Neither can one be sure of achieving the required standard of mental development merely by including a large number of problems in teaching, let alone the possible ambiguity of the problems. While trying to answer all these queries the researchers came across a number of ideas not directly related to the experiments in hand but rather to the topic we are discussing here. Such ideas may be summarized as follows: practically every piece of human knowledge, no matter what the field, is nothing but a well-tried solution to a well-known problem. There is no lack of such knowledge. Neither is there any lack of it in the curriculum. This knowledge provides a very poor basis for problem-solving and, besides, with much less material it would still be possible to teach creativity. But how can one teach the pupil to take his bearings in the ocean of knowledge and concentrate on tackling problems that he can really solve himself? It turned out that in each of the sciences that came under scrutiny (history, economic geography, languages, literature, chemistry) one could reduce the total of particular problems to a smaller number of typical problems, i.e. such problems that frequently arise in learning about any phenomenon in the matrix of a school subject. Typical problems were designated as 'on-going' or 'common'. The researchers reconciled themselves to the idea of teaching to solve a set of typical problems or to solve each type of problem. Upon analysing school subjects, each of them proved to contain a comparatively small number of on-going or common types (eight in economic geography, fifteen in history, eight in language study, etc.)[24]. These problems were broken down into groups and, upon analysing a few hundred items, it was confirmed that all the problem-solving situations could be arranged under group headings, every group being represented in the problems, and that there were no problems which fell outside these groups.

Cited below is the typology of common problems in economic geography compiled by Kovalevskaja[25]:

1. Definition and substantiation of a locality in terms of economic geography and the resulting effects on the structure of the economy;
2. Identification of links between the geographic environment and economic activity;
3. Identification of the level of economic development and the type of production.
4. Identification of the effects of distribution on the conditions of production;
5. Identification of forms of production and their economic effectiveness;
6. Identification of economic specialization in the local and national context;
7. Identification of economic specializations and the reasons for their distribution;
8. Identification of connections between industries in different regions.

Study material in economic geography should cover these eight aspects. The pupils should gradually become familiar with and learn to reproduce this pattern of eight aspects; problem-oriented methods are to be based on the pattern of the groups in each subject. Thus, a tool is provided for compiling the curriculum and textbook, as well as for actually teaching the pupils. Pupils in the senior classes adapt this pattern and apply it in other economic geography settings. Following the above typology, exercises are designed to reproduce the essential characteristics and problem-oriented methods that involve creative solutions. In other words, the group of common problems enables the compilation of teaching material incorporating all the four elements of curriculum content (see Chapter II).

Similar groupings compiled for other subjects lead, all other conditions being equal, to a tangible improvement in terms of intellectual development and depth of knowledge by relatively modest means. All this has been experimentally confirmed[26], but we wish to emphasize especially the role of grouping in selecting and subsequently constructing study material. These approaches cannot be expressed simply as verbal and visual information since they imply exercises and problem-solving methods. However, these are the means to acquire the patterns of reproductive and creative activity embodied in study material.

It is hardly possible to solve a problem without acquiring at the same time the *methods* to solve it. To this effect a study was undertaken to identify the methods of various sciences which could be used by the pupils and could form part of general education[27]. Thus, in the history course the pupils are taught to apply eleven different techniques. Listing these methods serves to guide the pupils' assignments, while the process of listing itself becomes part of subject content. Methods to solve common problems are formulated, and broken down into procedures and techniques to become objects of study.

A number of educational criteria to select curriculum content have had to be developed taking into consideration the fact that, as we have already said, content cannot be reduced to individual school subjects. Likewise, a number of activities have to be deliberately embodied in teaching content as specific units. A unit of instruction is the organized communication between the teacher and the pupils, communication which is subordinate to order and discipline. In the Soviet school such units are: a lesson, lecture, tutorial, debate, excursion or laboratory work. These units may be conducted with a whole class, a small group or with individual pupils. Each of these units assumes that the pupil will play different roles (group leader, consultant, discussion leader, participant, part of a team, etc.). Communicative skills are acquired at the class level and by involvement in smaller groups. The same skills are acquired through the patronage of junior classes by senior ones, and through activities conducted by the pupils at industrial enterprises and in the neighbourhood.

So much for didactic principles and criteria for the construction of subject content and curriculum content in general. The problem of selecting content is still far from being solved and further research is required.

4. TEXTBOOKS AND THE PRESENTATION OF CURRICULUM CONTENT

The educational rationales to select content, which were referred to in the preceding section, are to be used in compiling instructional programmes embodying curriculum content presented subject-by-subject. However, content is composed of blocks or units which are inventories of teaching objectives presented in a definite order of priority, even though the details of each unit may not be specified. Principles and criteria are important but not precise enough to select content for a textbook, which is a teaching document. A textbook presents content in terms of curricular units, but in a detailed form with regard to individual lessons and prescribing in broad outline the actual teaching process. In other words, a curriculum presents the nomenclature of content, indicates the order of priorities and the total scope of subject content, whereas a textbook expresses curriculum content in a logical sequence of homogenous units. In short, a textbook should express content to the point of actual teaching. We say 'should express', since in fact the clarity of expression will depend on the way the textbook has been conceived or on the actual interpretation of curriculum content. If content is reduced in the author's mind to knowledge, his textbook will more often than not simply present knowledge. If the function of a textbook is perceived only as the consolidation of the lesson, its content will be limited to a summary of the information in a lesson, sometimes even to the exclusion of questions which would evaluate the pupils' comprehension. Now that our view of curriculum content has been made clear, we set out to define the functions of a textbook in present-day classroom teaching.

Comprehensive education enrols a vast number of pupils from widely varying backgrounds and with different rates of acquisition. Therefore, a textbook should reflect these factors in the variety of its texts, the vividness of its narration and the presentation of questions. Even so, while aimed at different groups of pupils, the integrity of study material should be preserved.

The functions of a textbook can be specified still further by stating that the modern teaching process is still in the process of formation, still eluding mastery by many educators and that the best way to upgrade it for classroom use is to compile a textbook giving, as it were, a basic scenario of each lesson and each topic in hand. Experience shows that if a textbook does not contain any elements to develop intellectual ability, few teachers would pay any attention to this factor. A survey conducted on a sample of humanities textbooks[28] shows that, up to 1965, the assignments had mostly been of a reproductive nature. Reproductive teaching prevalent in school resulted from reproductively-written textbooks. After the ratio of productive to reproductive assignments in the textbooks had changed in favour of the former, the majority of teachers adopted the same pattern in their day-to-day practices. Teaching would have undergone little change had it not been for change in the textbook. One must even discount the contribution from professional literature on teaching methods, since intellectual capacity had already been stressed in methodology manuals for some time past, yet the contribution to change from this source proved less significant than that of textbooks.

The importance of a textbook can hardly be overestimated. Because the quality of teacher training cannot always be guaranteed and because of the lack of experience in student teachers, the textbook is an invaluable guide for beginning teachers when it comes to actual performance in the classroom. But even the most experienced of teachers cannot pretend to construct an adequately structured system of lessons which take into consideration all the necessary factors. Such a system is, however, within the reach of scholars adept not only at constructing curriculum content theoretically but also at expressing it in textbooks and other educational manuals.

The textbook is the principal medium for presenting the entire curriculum content for any school subject.

The textbook presents content at two levels: that of school subject and that of study material. The number of textbooks is determined by the need to cover the subject exhaustively (for example, the study of biology from the fifth to the tenth forms). On the other hand, every textbook also contains actual study material. But what is study material and how is it contained in the textbook? Up to now there has been no exhaustive definition of study material in the literature. Study material, just as curriculum content in general, has been regarded as no more than a set of knowledge.

It seems relevant to bring study material into line with the theoretical concept of curriculum content. It stands to reason that study material should include both knowledge and activities for the pupils by presenting assignments involving both, as well as the acquisition of creative behaviour patterns related to the topic under study, and desirable evaluative and emotional attitudes.

Study material should be laid down as clearly as possible, since it is the ultimate and most refined form of curriculum content. Study material should be defined not only as the content to be acquired, but also as that part of content which facilitates acquisition.

The latest findings of educational psychology and didactics favour the conclusion that the process of acquiring content (the ultimate goal of teaching) assumes the existence of an acquisition activity which must be present in the content and must be tailored to this content if it is to be acquired at all.

If, for instance, the teacher dwells upon the characteristics of an object, the pupils are supposed to be able to identify the dominant and secondary characteristics. If the teacher tells the pupils to establish these characteristics unaided using what they already know, they will have to base themselves on the analysis of that object. They must assemble the individual elements into a proper hierarchy, compare their knowledge with the task they have been given and express their conclusions. Thus, the group of activities for acquiring subject content has to include the activity of separating it into individual units of knowledge, describing them, ordering and comparing them, etc. And this newly acquired group of activities will in turn be incorporated into the content of teaching, and in this form it is bound to affect the time, method and level of acquisition. The acquisition of subject content is unthinkable without the mastery of logical thinking. Unless the pupil has grasped these practices at a level appropriate to the subject content and his age, he is likely to misinterpret the information and to acquire it in a purely mechanical way. Even if left out of the curriculum, these practices do find expression in the textbook in such forms as logical presentation, units replacing straight text and in the form of sequential units accompanying the actual text of subject content. Sandwiched among the practical units are various types of presentations (informative, illustrative, explicative, etc.). Textbook presentation should demonstrate the links between themes, their common origin, or the way they interact to transform, engender, develop or govern each other[29].

So far we have succeeded in elucidating only some of the elements of the study material, and it still remains for us to trace content in every detail by analysing the actual process of acquisition of any particular subject.

The problem consists of discovering all the forms in which the study material is reflected in a textbook. It is already abundantly clear that teaching activity could be effectively guided only after the most careful preparation of teaching units covering the smallest details of each school subject. This preparation must be duly, if only partly, reflected in the curriculum as a list of the required knowledge and types of activity. At the textbook level this content will find still more detailed expression through the gradual revelation of this knowledge, disclosing the links and providing assignments for the many activities concerned. Educational aids, such as encyclopedias, workbooks and assignment cards, also have a role to play. A film always provides visual and verbal information; it may either give 'ready-made' answers to the situations it presents or it may stimulate the pupils to search on their own.

A teachers' guide should throw considerable light on to the way curricular material is to be acquired. It should also include that part of the teacher's activity concerned with the organization of the pupils' learning activity.

Thus, study material may be defined as the content of activities aimed at the acquisition of curriculum content within a definite space of time.

What are the methods to embody curriculum content in textbooks? A survey of textbooks for various subjects, as well as other literature on the subject (published by Prosveščenie in its annual series *Problems of school textbooks*) favours the presentation of curriculum content in the form of texts, illustrations and notes (references, comments, footnotes, recommendations, etc.).

Modes of activity to be transformed into useful skills and habits are contained in a textbook as assignments for reproduction, located either prior to a text, in the text or in a concluding section.

Experience in creative activities can be gained through problem-solving questions, creative problems drawn from the text, or by referring to problems from other educational manuals and aids.

The content of aesthetic activities takes the form of interesting texts appealing to the reader's emotions through vividness in narration, illustrations, ingenious examples and presentations, by posing moral and aesthetic problems or assignments, or through expressing one's personal opinions or identifying one's personal system of values; in short, they require the pupil to react.

All the above-mentioned forms of including content in textbooks are self-evident and need no further comment. The real problem, as far as the pupil is concerned, is how to design and justify the order of priorities and sequence of these different methods of presentation. In other words, the composition of curriculum content determines the structure of a textbook in principle[30], yet in detail one may introduce variations. Presenting the structure of a textbook is a rather important problem which has to be resolved for each subject and group of subjects. The presentation of information in most countries is based upon a solid body of experience. Designing a proper system of assignments for textbooks is a more delicate matter, since it is supposed to describe both reproductive and original activity leading to an established pattern of action, during which time the pupil is also supposed to acquire knowledge. Here we are faced with a problem of correlating the content composition with a system of assignments, of providing principles on which to design assignments of a reproductive and original nature for textbooks in general. Lack of space prevents us from dealing in greater detail with a system of assignments. For the present, we limit our discussion to the impact the concept of curriculum content is likely to have on the problem of assignments in a textbook. Speaking about the connection between assignments and knowledge, it is worth noting that an assignment usually means activity and any activity connected with knowledge presupposes putting that knowledge into practice and hence the first (in order of priority) group of assignments may be designated as the *assignments for using knowledge*. In this particular case, we focus attention on the application of knowledge in the context of physics, history, etc. To design such a group of assignments, the textbook author should have very clear ideas about its basic concepts, whether first or second in priority, and about the links between them. Applying concepts, such as, for example, Ohm's Law, and analysing its influence assumes, firstly, learning the role of some concepts as a step towards learning the role of others and, secondly, identifying the situations in which concepts can be applied, bearing in mind the context of general secondary education and the intellectual development of the pupils. A good criterion for the first group of assignments is furnished by the set of situations in which knowledge is applied with reference to every topic.

Secondly, using knowledge means performing those practical and theoretical operations without which it is impossible to acquire knowledge. These operations can be acquired during the learning of each topic and frequently through extra-curricular content. The complete inventory of corresponding skills is an essential prerequisite to providing a complete range of assignments.

Both groups of assignments are divided into two further sub-groups: (a) stereotype assignments — reproduction of knowledge or activity patterns; (b) creative assignments — to develop the capacity to acquire and apply knowledge and modes of activity creatively, whether in practical or theoretical situations.

Thus, the entire complex of assignments connected with the composition of content may be divided into assignments for using knowledge after a pattern (or stereotype) and assignments for using knowledge creatively. The same applies to practical assignments. Assignments which belong to the same pattern, whether using knowledge or practical methods, should be integrated to save time and effort. Assignments, whether stereotyped or creative, should be designed exclusively by methodologists during the preparation of textbooks, since using knowledge is always subject-related and specific not only to a subject but also to a particular topic within a subject. The textbook author has the appropriate competence to decide which knowledge in the context of the given topic is to be used in a stereotyped way (reproduced) and which is to be used or procured by the pupil himself.

The practical activities suitable for each school subject (experiments, using a map, declension, working out dates, plotting graphs, workshop practice, etc.) are always selected by textbook authors. The practical activities common to all subjects are selected by educationists. Regretfully, the sample of textbooks surveyed by us contained a very limited number of such non-specific practical activities. Thus, the ones identified in the textbooks are: familiarization with an object (in real life, through models or by diagrams in a book); understanding and reproducing a text, breaking it down into elements (analysis), summarizing, comparing, giving examples, identifying the essential elements, definitions and explanations; establishing cause-and-effect connections, sizing up their relative importance and presenting them in a diagram. This is by no means an exhaustive inventory of what is to be selected for inclusion into the textbook. The practical activities mentioned in Chapter II partly make up for this gap, even though the inventory is, as yet, incomplete.

One should teach the pupils to size up the forms, importance, functions, causes, effects, purposes and composition of objects through assignments. Assignments should enable the pupil to learn to think in terms of purpose and means, part and whole, the subject and object of an action, the absolute and the relative, the general and the particular, the necessary and the fortuitous, contradictions, etc. The problem here is to correlate the subject-related content of assignments with activity. The subject-related content is governed by a definite logic, at least by that derived from the university entrance requirements, university textbooks, scientific compendia, whereas the (formal) logical and psychological content depends on a system composed of numerous factors such as age, acquisition capacity, the degree to which the material resists the logic of practical learning activities, etc. Compilation of a truly integrated textbook should be based on further and more profound research.

The designing of assignments on a number of topics was undertaken on a trial basis for the history course. As preparation for the history topic 'Formation of the Russian Empire in the early eighteenth century' for the seventh form, an inventory was made of main and subsidiary points. Upon rating the content of the topic and the receptiveness of the pupils, we determined which main and subsidiary points should be presented to the pupils as 'second-hand' knowledge and which should be discovered through the pupils' own research. Thereupon we identified the learning methods to be acquired while studying the topic. As a result a foundation was laid for designing assignments intended solely for the acquisition of subject-related content. From an initial distribution of assignments according to their form, experimental evaluation and final adjustment, we succeeded in classifying the assignments into stereotyped and creative types. Thereupon they were tested in actual classroom conditions. The designing of such assignments for the entire course of study and their division according to types and complexity of activity was a major contribution to the development of a system of assignments.

The content of study material is not an adequate criterion for the adequacy of assignments in each particular subject. The compiler should try to limit the number of assignments, particularly as the theorists do not encourage too many assignments per section of textbook. Their number can be appreciably curtailed by concentrating questions on a relatively few common problems (see Section 2).

Textbook assignments should, in principle, grow in complexity, though not necessarily in a gradual manner.

It is also advisable to include in textbooks assignments for developing evaluative and emotional capacity. In fact, any assignments can serve this purpose provided they take account of the needs of the pupils and their current attitudes. However, assignments serving this purpose can be made more specific. They serve to orient the pupils' needs in a socially useful direction and mould their system of values while further developing and orienting the system of values they already possess. These assignments are expected to train the pupils to assess their own knowledge, skills and activities; they are aimed at sensitizing the pupils' awareness to particular phenomena.

Thus, the whole complex of assignments in correlation with the content composition may be classified into assignments for acquiring learning skills, assignments for using knowledge and skills after a pattern, assignments for creatively using knowledge and skills, and assignments for developing moral attitudes. Knowledge and skills not directly related to knowledge may be integrated in the same assignments to save time and effort if they conform to the same pattern. The same is applicable to the assignments for reproductive and creative use of knowledge, on the one hand, and modes of activity, on the other. Using knowledge embodied in assignments, whether stereotyped or creative, is always specific not only to a particular subject but indeed to each particular topic within the subject. Attention has recently been paid, and quite reasonably so, to what is known as 'learning to learn' which is understood as methods to facilitate the pupil's own organization of his learning, methods which have little to do with the process of knowledge acquisition proper. Such learning skills include familiar operations like précis-writing, abstracting, etc. At present, these learning skills have been listed with a view to inclusion in curriculum content, and a certain number of them may well be embodied in textbooks. This point was mentioned earlier in Section 2.

Let us recapitulate what has been said in this section concerning the compilation of textbooks. The functions of a textbook are determined by the place it occupies in the system of educational planning. The course of studies as a whole is both the ultimate design and sum-total of means of teaching. This dualism of functions is also characteristic of a textbook; besides containing practical teaching material, it determines the teaching process. It is a very important means of teaching, since both the teacher and pupils use it in their work.

Textbooks, and instructional manuals in general, have acquired a new dimension in view of the trend towards structural integration, greater systematization of the normative sphere and the provision of more reliable foundations for teaching in general. In its role as just one element of the course of studies (which in turn comprises a sub-system of instruction as a whole), the textbook is tending to become part of a system and stands to lose some of its traditional role as the universal means of instruction. Even now, some of the functions of a textbook have been taken over by other documents such as teacher's guides, manuals and dictionaries, readers and anthologies, parallel texts to study foreign languages, pupils' study guides for unsupervised practice, notebooks with partly printed texts, etc. Other textbook functions are now performed by such materials as tables, pictures, drawings, audiovisual aids (films, slides, disk- and tape-recordings, TV and radio broadcasts, etc.), models, etc. Today, textbooks for foreign languages, history, geography and certain other subjects appear to be incomplete without audiovisual aids. An ever-greater role should be played in future by a complex of materials rather than by individual elements. This emerging structure, engendered by the tendency towards completeness and order, has to be taken into consideration when developing courses.

The proper place and function of a study book should also influence its content. Indeed, study books are now gaining a new status as the ultimate level in expressing both the content and process of instruction. Textbook material stands midway between the planned content and the content actually imparted during teaching. Thus, a system of assignments as part of study material is assembled by the author of a textbook and the same pattern of assignments is pursued by the teacher in the classroom. What takes place in the classroom implies the transformation of study material by the teacher as he prepares for a lesson, since he has to respect the actual conditions in which instruction is carried out in the classroom, such as the pupils' preparedness, their individual abilities, the teacher's own pattern of work, the pace of acquisition of material in related subjects, study-time available, etc.

The didactic rationales for constructing curriculum content — meaning textbook content — take the form of specific demands placed upon the study material. These demands may be embodied in the textbook as various parts of the content, such as the methods to present the main and supplementary units of knowledge, the criteria for the range and complexity of study material. At the same time, general didactic norms serve as guidelines at all levels of compiling curriculum content. At the level of giving substance to curriculum content, didactic guidelines keep one's attention fixed on the essential points which should be borne in mind. When an author is faced with the problem of presenting the material of a school subject in a textbook, he is likely to be concerned that the material not only conforms to the most recent advances on the subject but also to the agreed teaching situations and instructional forms. Then teaching will be perceived by the textbook author as an object of construction, which means paying attention to the educational and methodological regularities identified through the study of teaching.

5. LINKS BETWEEN CURRICULUM THEORY AND INSTRUCTION

Earlier in this book we discussed the application of the theory of curriculum content to the practical construction of that content in general and in its embodiment in school subjects in particular. However, the role of this theory does not end there. The theoretical conceptualization of curriculum content involves the expression of those problems of teaching theory which have a decisive influence on teaching practice, i.e. where content is employed.

It is thanks to the theory of curriculum content that teaching activity and instructional methods are now better understood. For instance, it has now become possible to clarify and to describe with more precision, and perhaps one day to obtain a solution to, the chronic problem of the ratio of instruction-to-development. No less challenging appears to be the problem of the ratio of objective-to-subjective elements in the activity of a teacher, and the limits he may go to in creating and improving the content. For lack of space we cannot go into the details of these difficulties and we will restrict our discussion to the most important solutions to date.

The first of these, theoretically conducive to the understanding of others, is a problem of the links between curriculum content and the teaching process. To clarify the essence of the problem we must say a few words about how we understand the instructional process.

Content comes twice into contact with the instructional process. The first time it happens is at the level of curriculum and textbooks. Content cannot be considered to exist until the curriculum and textbooks have been evaluated. In other words, content embodied in school syllabuses (subject content) can be accepted as a blueprint for teaching only upon its confirmation in an actual classroom situation.

The next encounter of content with teaching occurs when the blueprint is introduced extensively. The first encounter, of a heuristic nature, is thus aimed at constructing an optimum content blueprint, whereas the second has the purpose of getting the younger generation ready to perform as individuals in society.

What are the characteristics of the process of instruction?

The source of teaching as a functioning social institution is the need of society to pass on to the younger generation social experience. For this to become attainable the social goals of instruction have to be embodied in curriculum content. Curriculum content is the means whereby the teacher carries on the activity of teaching, with due regard to the pupils' motivation and to providing them with motivation to learn. Once the motives and aims of the pupils have been aligned with those of the teacher, teaching may begin, i.e. the mechanism is set in motion whereby content is being acquired. If the mechanisms and practices of acquisition are disregarded, teaching assumes an empirical, superficial and wasteful character. Once the mechanism of acquisition is working, there is a result, i.e. the conversion of part of social experience into part of the pupil's personality. The result is evaluated by the teacher who has thus expended a current portion of content, i.e. study material, before starting on the next act of instruction. These acts make up the process of instruction.

The instructional process consists of the following components: goals placed upon education by society; curriculum content; teacher/pupil interaction and the means used to maintain it (teaching methods; the pupils' motivation through which the teacher imparts to them his intentions and they in turn align their activity with these intentions; the mechanism and outcome of acquisition; the feedback justifying each successive act of instruction). All these components are inevitably contained within the instructional process, and their interconnections have a definite structure the study of which results in several conclusions. These components, as they are presented above, are characteristic of instruction in general, yet this process is historically variable, every epoch having had a particular impact. But what we want to know is when does a change in one element bring about a decisive change in the character of teaching, whether for the entire epoch or for a particular moment, since one is dealing here with a dynamic system in constant turmoil.

It stands to reason that an element which has a decisive influence is one that is represented by a modification of social demands and educational goals. These are subject to change through social development. They serve as the source of teaching and the reason for its existence; they determine curriculum content and any change therein; and, last but not least, they influence the motivations of the teacher as a representative of society. And yet, a social goal cannot be considered as the component which causes the education system to change. To perform this function successfully, i.e. to change educational goals, social goals must be translated into educational terms or, in other words, into the language of curriculum content. Any goal of education can be achieved if it is included in advance in an appropriate programme of activity and if that programme can be acquired by the pupils on a properly organized basis. In the USSR, the goals of secondary education, and hence education in general, are understood as the moulding of comprehensively educated, socially active citizens with an objective and progressive outlook, with an honest attitude to work, healthy, capable of performing successfully in various economic, social and cultural fields, actively participating in local and national affairs, staunchly defending their country, preserving and augmenting the material and cultural heritage, and conserving the natural environment. Soviet public education gives citizens the possibility of developing and satisfying their cultural and intellectual needs. Any of these goals — serving as a guide and principle to construct curriculum content — is attainable solely through their expression in knowledge, modes of activity and a system of values and needs. In the absence of this content acquired through teaching, these goals are not attainable.

Curriculum content reflecting the social goals of teaching is that key component which integrates the teaching process into a system. Through teaching, content performs the functions of aim, means, object and outcome. As we have already pointed out, curriculum content is an educational expression of social goals. Besides, in the form of study material it is also the purpose of the teacher's teaching activity. At every moment of teaching the teacher is contriving to encourage the pupils to acquire each current portion of the lesson. The teacher's activity is focused upon the attainment of this aim which is a step, limited in time, towards the attainment of the general goal of education.

For the teacher curriculum content is a means to achieve the goal, since it is through the study material that the teacher organizes the pupils' activity and selects means of teaching appropriate to that material (verbal presentation, drawing, experiment, technical demonstration, etc.).

For the pupil, curriculum content is something to be acquired and it is in this process that the practices of acquisition come into use.

And finally, curriculum content becomes an outcome of the teaching process once it has been acquired — and in the form in which it has been acquired. In the role of outcome it becomes a characteristic of personality, a stage in the teaching process, a prerequisite to the next stage. For explanation's sake we have described the functions of content one by one, but in fact they operate simultaneously.

There is more to say on the role curriculum content plays in the educational process.

The important role of curriculum content in the instructional process determines the very logic of that process, its consistency in progressing towards a goal. This needs some explanation.

Curriculum content being heterogeneous in its composition (knowledge, activity methods, etc.), each of its elements has to be acquired in a specific manner. In the initial stages, the acquisition of knowledge depends on consciously perceiving and memorizing information received through all the senses. To acquire skills and useful habits, i.e. activities presented by the teacher, one way or another the pupils have to reproduce these methods repeatedly. To acquire experience in creativity it is absolutely essential to take part in solving problem-oriented assignments. The acquisition of a personal attitude, i.e. the acquisition of experience in establishing one's own moral response, is attained through the pupil responding emotionally to the study material, in other words, through teaching which is motivating.

Knowing the particular methods of acquiring various types of curriculum content enables the appropriate teaching methods to be pinpointed. A teaching method can be defined as a system of actions on the part of the teacher to organize the pupils' practical and learning activity, and to get them to acquire curriculum content[31].

Since curriculum content consists of four dissimilar elements, each of which is acquired by a different method, teaching methods should also vary in accordance with the content element and the method of its acquisition — a process to be organized by the teacher. Thus, to enable the initial acquisition of information received through all the senses, it is absolutely essential to use an *explanatory illustrative method*. At this stage, the perception, comprehension and memorization of information by pupils is entirely supervised. This is achieved through the tactile, visual, auditory and other kinds of perception, the manipulation of objects or their models, discussion, drawing or observing natural objects. The pupil performs learning activity through practical activity, i.e. through manipulating the actual object to be learned, watching pictures or films, listening to the teacher telling a story or reading a passage from a textbook, understanding what he perceives and committing it to memory.

To acquire modes of activity and to transform them into skills and useful habits one has to use a *reproductive method*. This consists of the teacher (with or without teaching aids) getting the pupils either to imitate or modify previously demonstrated actions. The reproductive method is exemplified in exercises in writing, reading, storytelling, problem-solving, operating a machine tool.

To acquire experience in creative activity one resorts to methods of problem-oriented teaching, under which the pupils are supposed to solve problems more or less unsupervised.

The principal method of problem-oriented teaching is a *discovery method*. It consists in the teacher designing a system of problems with pre-set parameters[32] which the pupils are expected to solve on their own, thereby displaying and enriching their creative experience.

Experience in creative activity is acquired step-by-step in keeping with the pattern followed in learning about a complicated object. In other words, this is done by a *heuristic method*. When the pupil is assigned a problem, the teacher first divides it into sub-problems and, through a process of helpful hints, leads the pupil to the solution, thus preserving its problem-oriented character. Another method consists of a sequence of questions most of which depend for an answer on creative guesswork and each of which is a step towards the final solution.

And finally, another method of problem-oriented teaching is known as *guided discovery*. It consists of the teacher posing a problem and himself solving it, but in the process he demonstrates the contradictions encountered, thus drawing attention to the complexity in learning about certain situations. During this process the pupils cannot help following the teacher's reasoning, thus becoming involved in finding the solution, whether in thought or in deed, expressing doubts or suggestions. In this way, they are not merely perceiving information, including that concerning the learning process, but indeed by taking a part in it are guided to a level of reasoning which is compatible with their intellect.

These methods include all the known teaching techniques. But beyond this, to make these methods really work, one has to pay heed to the pupils' motivation and emotional attitudes; and one must ensure that content and methods are correlated with the pupils' desire to know, communicate, fulfil and assert themselves. In using these methods, one resorts to several means (verbal, visual, practical) or their combination in packages, but, be that as it may, the main distinction of a method remains the degree to which the learning activity corresponds to the content. All the other distinguishing traits (means, forms, packages) are common to all the elements of curriculum content. Their specificity does not go beyond teaching. Thus, it is curriculum content that determines the selection of teaching methods and hence the form of the teaching process. In broad outline, the logic of instruction follows the basic pattern of getting the pupil to acquire information on the object under study in class. The pupil then reproduces the patterns of activity in order to apply the acquired knowledge in similar situations, thus acquiring the appropriate skills and habits. This is followed by the application of the knowledge and skills in new circumstances, which involves a creative approach. Throughout all these consecutive stages the pupil is given motivation, trained to react emotionally to the subject being taught and to participate in the learning process.

While learning content, the pupil may have to use different acquisition techniques, which assumes the use of different teaching methods — the different combinations depending on previously acquired content.

The logic of unfolding the instructional process is invariably determined by the way the elements comprising curriculum content are combined. This combination determines the logic of organizing acquisition techniques, the sequence of teaching methods and the rhythm of the acquisition mechanism. Indeed, curriculum content has its own characteristics which determine the pupil's acquisition activity and the teacher's organizing activity. This explains the connection between teaching methods and curriculum content.

Curriculum content in the above explanation also includes the function of instruction which should find an optimum ratio between instruction and intellectual development. It can be claimed with certainty that knowledge and modes of activity imparted to the pupil 'second-hand' do not stimulate intellectual development in keeping with the expectations of modern society. They merely serve to enable a grasp of a few intellectual and cognitive patterns applicable to a few stereotyped or familiar situations. The range of their transfer to new situations is strictly limited.

To apply acquired knowledge and skills in original situations, in a habitual and independent manner, the pupil needs more stimulation. The pupil needs to acquire experience in creative activity, experience in visualizing a problem, in imagining a novel function for a familiar object, in analysing the structure of an object, in alternative reasoning and the other patterns of creative thinking (see Chapter II), which, it will be remembered, cannot be inculcated through the conventional methods of acquiring knowledge and skills. Intellectual development leading to independent organization of one's own practical and mental activities in order to cope with the most challenging problems involves the acquisition of not only stereotyped knowledge and behaviour but also experience in the creative activity of transforming knowledge. Indeed, it requires something out of the ordinary — imparting curriculum content to the pupil in all its complexity, each element varying in its origins in social experience and in its contribution to socio-cultural and personality development. In short, instruction also means intellectual development, provided it draws upon *all* the elements of curriculum content and not merely on stereotyped knowledge and habitual behaviour. The acquisition of all the elements of content, the proper degree of consolidation and measures to carry out frequent evaluation, can well be expected to solve the problem of moulding members of society who not only know something or know how to do something but also possess an adequate degree of intellectual and cultural development.

The links between curriculum content and the other components of instruction can be described as feedback. In other words, the components of instruction in turn affect specific portions of curriculum content. Thus, content is affected by teaching methods, the rate of acquisition, teacher/pupil and pupil/pupil relationships, and teaching forms in each particular case. This interaction being obvious enough, our interest is focused on those portions of curriculum content which are affected by the above components of the instructional process, a problem already touched upon earlier in this book.

Curriculum content, the embodiment of the goals of instruction, determines the process of instruction or rather its unfolding. The teacher's aims are determined by content and thus his activity is derived from the acquisition practices he chooses to employ. By determining acquisition methods, content also determines the pupils' activity and how well they are motivated. Motivation is more particularly determined by the compatibility between the teacher's activity and their actual needs. Content determines the selection of the means of instruction from the sum-total available. Content shares with the learner's activity the determination of mechanisms of acquisition. And finally, content serves as a yardstick to estimate the results of teaching and, upon its acquisition by the pupils, it indicates the next step of instruction.

Besides curriculum content, other components of the teaching process play a role but, firstly, that role is derived from content and, secondly, we are above all interested in finding connections between curriculum content and the teaching process.

The long and the short of it all is that curriculum content is the main prerequisite to attaining the goals of education and socialization. Thus, it is the theoretical conceptualization of content, its composition, the links between its elements and how each element functions that should, hopefully, bring about a solution to the problems confronting formal education in Soviet society.

Furthermore, this theoretical discussion poses quite a few educational problems which call for practical measures to improve curriculum content and the resultant education and socialization imparted in school.

The first problem in order of priority and complexity appears to be that of optimizing the minimum content to be acquired on finishing elementary, incomplete secondary and complete secondary school. This minimum should cover knowledge and skills, as well as work-oriented, physical, social and ethical education.

The second problem is how to include the elements of content in the curriculum and syllabuses.

The third problem is that of compiling an adequate curriculum for all types of secondary comprehensive school.

The fourth problem is that of arriving at the correct proportioning between the natural sciences and the humanities.

The fifth problem is that of providing adequate teaching methods for each school subject, which means furnishing methodological guidelines with due regard to all the possible variations.

The sixth problem is that of compiling adequate textbooks, structuring them properly and embodying the various elements of curriculum content.

The seventh problem is that of identifying how far the teacher may go in improvising upon the core curriculum in order to bring it into line with the dynamics of the classroom.

The eighth problem is to establish evaluation techniques for testing in actual classroom conditions curricula and textbooks which have been established according to theoretical procedures.

*   *   *

We cannot pretend to have covered all the problems pertaining to curriculum content. The present discussion is not concerned with the problems pertaining to teaching itself. However, even comparing the components of the instructional process with those of curriculum content is sufficient to identify those problems which are subject to analysis at didactic and methodological levels.

Still another problem of consequence to the organizers and practitioners of education is that of the mastery by teachers, administrators and researchers of an integral didactic approach to the analysis, evaluation and organization of the actual process of teaching.

It is the educational culture of the decision maker that should, in the final analysis, determine the level of the actual performance of our school. But the school obviously stands in need of an adequate educational theory to be equal to satisfying the demands placed by modern society on formal education.

REFERENCES

1. Hirst, P.H.; Peters, R.S. *The logic of education.* London, Routledge & Kegan Paul, 1970, p. 60.
2. Ivin, A.A. *Logika norm.* Moskva, Izdatel'stvo Moskovskogo universiteta, 1973, p. 21.
3. See: Žuravlev, I.K.; Zorina, L.Ja. Didaktičeskaja model' učebnogo predmeta. *Novye issledovanija v pedagogičeskih naukah* (Moskva), no. 1(33), 1979.
4. See: Lerner, I.Ja. Sostav soderžanija obrazovanija i puti ego voploščenija v učebnike. *In:* Zankov, L.V., et al. *Problemy škol'nogo učebnika.* Moskva, Prosveščenie, 1978. (Voprosy teorii učebnika, vyp. 6).
5. See: Vysockaja, S.I. Didaktičeskie osnovanija opredelenija sistemy umenij i navykov v gumanitarnyh učebnyh predmetah. *Novye issledovanija v pedagogičeskih naukah* (Moskva), no. 1(37), 1981.
6. See: Vysockaja, S.I. Učebnye zatrudnenija kak sredstvo proverki kačestva znanij. *In:* Skatkin, M.N.; Krasovskij, V.V., eds. *Kačestvo znanij učaščihsja i puti ego soveršenstvovanija.* Moskva, 'Pedagogika', 1978.
7. See: Kuz'mina, N.V. *Očerki psihologii truda učitelja.* Leningrad, Izdatel'stvo Leningradskogo universiteta, 1967.
8. See: Zuev, D.D. Problemy programmirovanija aktivizacii didakti☐ skih funkcij sovremennogo škol'nogo učebnika v processe ego sozdanija. *In:* Babanskij, Ju.K., et al. *Problemy škol'nogo učebnika.* Moskva, 'Prosveščenie', 1980, p. 274-277. (Voprosy teorii učebnika, vyp. 8).
9. Kagan, M.S. *Čelovečeskaja dejatel'nost'.* Moskva, 1974.

10. Lerner, I.Ja. *Process obučenija i ego zakonomernosti.* Moskva, Znanie, 1980.
11. Krevnevič, B.B. *Vlijanie naučno-tehničeskogo progressa na izmenenija struktury rabočego klassa SSSR.* Moskva, 1971.
12. Zorina, L.Ja. Konkretizacija principa naučnosti v didaktike. *Novye issledovanija v pedagogičeskih naukah* (Moskva), no. 13(26), 1975.
13. Zorina, L.Ja. *Didaktičeskie osnovy formirovanija sistemnosti znanij staršeklassnikov.* Moskva, 'Pedagogika', 1978. 128 p.
14. Lednev, V.S. *Soderžanie obščego srednego obrazovanija: problemy struktury.* Moskva, 1980.
15. Žuravlev, I.K.; Zorina, L.Ja. Didaktičeskaja model' učebnogo predmeta. *Novye issledovanija v pedagogičeskih naukah* (Moskva), no. 2(32), 1978.
16. *Sovetskaja pedagogika* (Moskva), no. 3, 1979; no. 1, 1970.
17. Cetlin, V.S. *Neuspevaemost' škol'nikov i ee predupreždenie.* Moskva, 'Pedagogika', 1977. 120 p.
18. Zorina, *Didaktičeskie ..., op.cit.*
19. *Ibid.*
20. *Ibid.*
21. Lerner, I.Ja., ed. *Poznavatel'nye zadači v obučenii gumanitarnym naukam.* Moskva, 'Pedagogika', 1972. 239 p.
22. Mahmutov, M.I. *Problemnoe obučenie: osnovnye voprosy teorii.* Moskva, 'Pedagogika', 1975. 21 p.
23. Matjuškin, A.M. *Problemnye situacii v myšlenii i obučenii.* Moskva, 'Pedagogika', 1972. 208 p.
24. Lerner, *Poznavatel'nye ..., op.cit.*
25. Lerner, *op.cit.,* p. 209.
26. Lerner, I.Ja. Poisk dokazatel'stv i poznavatel'naja samostojatel'nost' učaščihsja. *Sovetskaja pedagogika* (Moskva), no. 7, 1974, p. 28-37.
27. Lerner, Poznavatel'nye zadiči, *op.cit.*
28. *Ibid.*
29. Blauberg, I.V.; Judin, E.G. *Stanovlenie i sušnost' sistemnogo podhoda.* Moskva, 1973, p. 188-190.
30. Lerner, Sostav soderžanija obrazovanija, *op.cit.*
31. Lerner, I.Ja. Didaktičeskie osnovy metodov obučenija. Moskva, 1981.
32. Lerner, *Poznavatel'nye ..., op.cit.*